BLOOD SIMPLE & RAISING ARIZONA

by the same authors

BARTON FINK & MILLER'S CROSSING
THE HUDSUCKER PROXY
FARGO

Blood Simple
&
Raising Arizona

JOEL COEN and ETHAN COEN

faber and faber

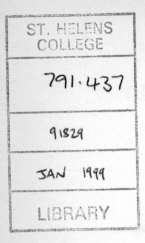
First published in separate volumes in the United States in 1988
By St Martin's Press, 175 Fifth Avenue,
New York, New York 10010
First published in the UK in 1996
by Faber and Faber Limited
3 Queen Square London WC1N 3AU

Printed in England by Clays Ltd, St Ives plc

A CIP record for this book
is available from the British Library

ISBN 0–571–19090–1

2 4 6 8 10 9 7 5 3 1

Contents

Blood Simple

Preface

"What was your shooting ratio?"

It is a question often asked at festival and college screenings of our movies. The question means, how did the total footage shot compare to the total footage of the completed picture? For some reason the question fascinates people the world over, while other pointlessly precise questions are never asked. No one asks about our teamster ratio, for instance, which compares the total number of teamsters employed on the picture to the number of teamsters who worked. Nor does anyone ask about our paper ratio, which compares the total number of pages of notes and drafts to the hundred or so pages of finished screenplay manuscript. But the fact that no one is interested enough to ask doesn't preclude our answering, and we have chosen this last question as our theme.

A reader of the finished script to which these remarks serve as prolegomenon might well wonder, if this is the stuff they thought was good enough to shoot, what could they possibly have thrown out? Fair question, and we will shortly provide a sample. First, however, we would like to point out that, excepting present remarks, virtually all written material underwent a process of revision and redrafting. This is a time-honored tradition and among professional writers it carries no stigma and is not considered "cheating." Rarely is the reading public given the opportunity to inspect an author's mucilaginous crude before it is refined and transmuted into what Heinrich Heine once called "gaz." Few realize, for instance, that the first draft of Herman Melville's grand meditation on the vasty deep began, "Just call me Ishmael." In revision, fortunately, the bearded bard of the bounding main deleted his chef d'oeuvre's first word; we may be grateful also that Pittsfield's Homer expanded the name of his eponymous behemoth from the first draft's folksy but retentive "Dick."

How fortunate that, in sculpting one of his classic sonnets, Shakespeare applied so ruthless a chisel to the first draft:

> When to the sessions of sweet silent thought
> We summon up remembrance of things from a long time
> ago . . .

In the first draft of *Macbeth*, the Bard of Avon had his gloomy Gael reflect on life:

> It is a tale told by an idiot
> Full of sound and fury
> And all manner of things.

Sensing room for improvement, the author concocted a new epiphany for his dyspeptic highlander:

> It is a tale told by an idiot
> Full of sound and fury
> Nor meaneth it a thing.

In the third draft, the poet put these words into the mouth of his henpecked Scot:

> *It is a tale told by an egret*
> *Full of sound and fury*
> *Signifying nothing.*

Well, one step forward, one step back.

And so it was with *Blood Simple*. For instance, in an early draft of the script, Ray, the befuddled bartender who for want of a more compelling character served as our story's hero, fled the scene of the tale's protracted central murder and checked into a motel outside of San Antonio:

MOTEL LOBBY DAY

DUSTY RHODES, a lean man with a weathered face and large Adam's apple, stands behind the Formica check-in counter. KYLE, a heavyset man of thirty wearing a feed cap, sits in the lobby's one piece of furniture, a beat-up leatherette sofa. He sips from a can of soda.

RAY, begrimed and haggard, enters out of the glare of the noonday sun.

RHODES: Hey there, stranger! What can I do you for?

RAY: I need a room.

Calling out from the divan:

KYLE: He needs a room, Dusty.

RHODES: I reckon I can hear him . . .

. . . (*to RAY*) Room rate's eight sixty-six a day plus sales tax, plus extra for the TV option.

RAY: How much extra?

KYLE (*calling out*):   He wants the TV option, Dusty.

RHODES: I reckon I can hear him. TV option, that's a dollar twenty, makes nine eighty-six plus tax.

KYLE (*calling out*):   Tell him the channels, Dusty.

RHODES: Channels, we got two and six. Two don't come in so hot.

RAY: Just a room then.

KYLE (*calling out*):   He don't want the option, Dusty.

RHODES: I reckon I heard the man.

RAY (*after shooting* KYLE *an irritated glance*):   Does he work here?

KYLE (*calling out*):   Sure don't.

RHODES: See, Wednesday's the special on RC Cola. I don't know if I explained about the TV option. If there's a TV in the room, you got to pay the option.

KYLE (*calling out*):   And how many rooms got TV, Dusty?

RHODES: Ever durned one.

RAY (*gamely*):   Okay, I'll take the TV option.

RHODES: Well see the thing about that is, we're booked.

Looking at this scene now, years later, it strikes us that revising it out of existence, as we did, constituted too much rewriting. Indeed, the more prosaic scene we replaced it with, involving Ray stopped at a traffic light, can be found in the finished script but not in the finished movie. It was shot but then deleted in order to more quickly get to the carnage, which was the picture's raison d'être.

In fact—for those of you who have seen the movie—in an early draft of the climactic scene the heroine, after impaling the private detective's hand on the window sill, saws off his captive fingers and pops them through the holes that he has shot into the wall that separates them. An even earlier draft had her first pull the nails off the disembodied fingers with a grimping hook, but we were advised that this might frighten small children.

So finally, by trimming the script instead of the digits of our hapless private snoop, we arrived at the paradigm of restraint that is now the climax of the movie. "Sell-out!" some people will say. But one must remember that Art and Commerce are uneasy bedfellows 'neath picturedom's sheets, nor may they even shake hands without spraining something.

But we mentioned earlier that we were "advised" in this matter, which brings us to another aspect of the writing process.

Young writers just starting out and eager to make good should know that the world teems with critics—ugly, bitter people, fat and acned for the most part, often afflicted with gout, dropsy, and diseases of the inner ear. Always they know better; always they recognize just exactly what is missing; always, always they can point the way to a finer choice.

That is why, on occasion, we search them out. But beware: Though the critic can tell you how to improve, he will never tell you what is equally important, when to stop improving. The critic is a lonely man, and a crafty one.

He knows that if he tells you your work is finished,

then you will also be finished listening to him; and so he indefatigably navigates, while you long for a sign that your voyage is over—as does, no doubt, the traveler through these remarks. Dizzied and dazed by a lack of organization, he himself back now, Magellanlike, at the point of origin. What was our paper ratio? How much rewriting is enough? How much is too much? When do you quit?

Even did he wish to, the critic couldn't answer, for he doesn't know. He might believe that you quit revising a manuscript when it is "right." He might also believe that a bell sounds on the floor of the stock exchange when the Dow has reached its high for the day. Neither will the professional writer tell you the rule for when to stop writing, because he is insecure, fearful of giving up trade secrets and losing his competitive edge. *We'll* tell you, because we're in the movie business and so our careers depend upon public caprice rather than on the play of competitive market forces. The rule is, you quit rewriting when your manuscript starts to bore you. Only the amateur, who has boundless energy and who lacks the imagination to quit, ever works beyond that point.

Consult, then, your heart. Once your work feels stale and tiresome you should present it to the public. Anyway, that's what we do.

J.C. and E.C.
New York
August 1988

Credits

The Players

Ray	John Getz
Abby	Frances McDormand
Julian Marty	Dan Hedaya
Private Detective	M. Emmet Walsh
Meurice	Samm-Art Williams
Debra	Deborah Neumann
Landlady	Raquel Gavia
Man from Lubbock	Van Brooks
Mr. Garcia	Señor Marco
Old Cracker	William Creamer
Strip Bar Exhorter	Loren Bivens
Strip Bar Senator	Bob McAdams
Stripper	Shannon Sedwick
Girl on Overlook	Nancy Finger
Radio Evangelist	Rev. William Preston Robertson

Directed by	Joel Coen
Produced by	Ethan Coen
Written by	Joel Coen and Ethan Coen
Executive Producer	Daniel F. Bacaner
Associate Producer	Mark Silverman
Director of Photography	Barry Sonnenfeld
Production Designer	Jane Musky
Music by	Carter Burwell
Edited by	Roderick Jaynes and
	Don Wiegmann
First Assistant Director	Deborah Reinisch

Credits

Casting	Julie Hughes and Barry Moss
Special Effects Coordinator	Loren Bivens
Location Manager and Austin Casting	Edith M. Clark
Second Assistant Director	Steve Love
Third Assistant Director	Shannon Wood
Location Coordinator	Don Hartack
Production Office Coordinator	Alma Kuttruff
Assistant to Production Designer	Steve Roll
Property Master	Shirley Belwood
Property Assistant	Marcos E. Gonzalez
Focus Puller	David Frederick
Clapper/Loader	Don Kirk
Sound Mixer	Lee Orloff
Boom	Peter F. Kurland
Gaffer	Joey Forsyte
Second Electric	Julie Gant
Electricians	Don Wiegmann
	John Shaw
Key Grip	Tom Prophet, Jr.
Best Boy	Richard Creasy
Third Grip	Angelo Suasnovar
Make-Up	Jean Ann Black
Wardrobe Designers	Sara Medina-Pape
	Chelle Coleman
Script Supervisor	Andreas Laven
Location Editor	Peggy Connolly
Special Effects Make-Up and Prosthetics	Paul R. Smith
Special Effects Mechanical	Michael K. O'Sullivan
Set Dresser	Nancy Griffith
Art Department Assistants	Bob Sturtevant
	Jeff Adams
	Michael Peal
	Kathy Baker
	Dave Pearce
Special Graphics	Beth Parry
Photo Retoucher	David Wander
Special Stills	Blaine Pennington
Editorial Consultant	Edna Ruth Paul
Sound Editors	Skip Lievsay
	Michael R. Miller

CREDITS

Special Sound Effects	Fred Szymanski
	Jun Mizumachi
Music Coordinator and Production	Murri Barber
Re-recording Mixer	Mel Zelniker
Location Auditor	H. Harris Willcockson
Dog Trainer	Marty Mahoney
Dialect Coach	Lizanne Brazell
Casting Associates	Peter Golden
	Phil DiMaggio
Negative Cutter	Victor Concepcion
Title Design	Dan Perri
Production Assistants	Van Brooks
	Ingrid Weigand
	David McGill
	Melanie Hecht
	Webster Lewin
	Darrell Kreitz
	Adam Smith
	John Woodward
	Richard Woolsey
	Shawn Malone
	Tom Martin
Color by	DuArt
Post-Production Services by	The Spera Corporation and Sound One Corporation
Optical Effects by	The Optical House, New York
Special Thanks to	Hilary Ney
	Earl Miller
	Ivan Bigley
	Renaissance Pictures
	Ron Seres
	George Majesski
	C. Wilson Interiors
	Abel Stationers
	Computerland of Austin
	Texas Film Commission

Shot on Location in Austin and Hutto, Texas

LANDSCAPES

An opening voice-over plays against dissolving Texas landscapes—broad, bare, and lifeless.

VOICE-OVER: The world is full of complainers. But the fact is, nothing comes with a guarantee. I don't care if you're the Pope of Rome, President of the United States, or even Man of the Year—something can always go wrong. And go ahead, complain, tell your problems to your neighbor, ask for help—watch him fly.

Now in Russia, they got it mapped out so that everyone pulls for everyone else—that's the theory, anyway. But what I know about is Texas . . .

CUT TO:
ROAD   NIGHT

We are rushing down a rain-swept country road, listening to the rhythmic swish of tires on wet asphalt.

And down here . . . you're on your own.

INT   CAR   NIGHT

We are looking at the backs of two people in the front seat—a man, driving, and a woman next to him.

Their conversation will be punctuated by the occasional glare of oncoming headlights and the roar of the car rushing by.

The windshield wipers wave a soporific beat. The conversation is halting, awkward.

WOMAN: . . . He gave me a little pearl-handled .38 for our first anniversary.

MAN: Uh-huh.

WOMAN: . . . Figured I'd better leave before I used it on him. I don't know how you can stand him.

MAN: Well, I'm only an employee, I ain't married to him.

WOMAN: Yeah . . .

Pause, as an oncoming car passes. Finally:

. . . I don't know. Sometimes I think there's something wrong with him. Like maybe he's sick? Mentally? . . . Or is it maybe me, do you think?

MAN: Listen, I ain't a marriage counselor. I don't know what goes on, I don't wanna know . . . But I like you. I always liked you . . .

Another car passes.

. . . What're you gonna do in Houston?

WOMAN: I'll figure something out . . . How come you offered to drive me in this mess?

MAN: I told you. I like you.

WOMAN: See, I never knew that.

MAN: Well now you do.

WOMAN: . . . Hell.

Another pause, another car.
  Suddenly:

WOMAN: Stop the car, Ray!

CLOSE SHOT   BRAKE
Stamped on.

EXT   CAR
Low three-quarters on the car as it squeals to a halt.
  A car that has been following screeches to a halt just behind it.
  Both cars sit.
  Rain patters.

INT   FIRST CAR
Close on the man, from behind.
  He looks at the woman.

MAN: . . . Abby?

She doesn't answer. He turns to look back and we see his face, for the first time, in the headlights of the car behind.

HIS POV
The car behind them waiting, patiently. Rain drifts down past its headlights.

Finally it pulls out and passes them slowly, their headlights showing it to be a battered green Volkswagen. First the car itself, then its red taillights, disappear into the rain.

BACK TO THE MAN

Cutting between him and the woman, each from behind.

MAN: . . . You know that car?

WOMAN: No.

MAN: What's the matter?

WOMAN: I don't know . . . I just think maybe I'm making a mistake . . .

She looks at the man.

. . . What was that back there?

MAN: Back where.

WOMAN: Sign.

MAN: I don't know. Motel . . . Abby—

WOMAN: Ray. Did you mean that, what you said before, or were you just being a gentleman?

MAN: Abby, I like you, but it's no point starting anything now.

WOMAN: Yeah.

MAN: I mean, I ain't a marriage counselor—

WOMAN: Yeah.

The man is uncomfortable.

MAN: . . . What do you want to do?

The woman is uncomfortable. After a long pause:

WOMAN: . . . What do *you* want to do?

MOTEL ROOM

Pulling back from RAY *and* ABBY *in bed, making love.*
The only light is from cars passing along the highway
outside. Each sweeping light-by ends in black.
The pullback ends in a wide shot of the motel room. The
black following the last car-by lingers.
A telephone rings.

SAME WIDE SHOT   MORNING

RAY *and* ABBY *are asleep. On a nightstand next to the bed,*
the telephone is ringing.
RAY *stirs, reaches for the phone.*

RAY: . . . Hello.

VOICE: Having a good time?

RAY: . . . What? Who is this?

VOICE: I don't know, who's this?

A silence at both ends.

. . . You still there?

RAY: Yeah, I'm still here.

RAY *listens to another silence. It ends with a disconnect.*
    ABBY *is stirring as* RAY *gets out of bed.*

ABBY: . . . Ray?

RAY: Yeah.

ABBY: What was that?

RAY: Your husband.

BAR BACK OFFICE   NIGHT

*We are tracking past a man seated behind a wooden desk,
towards an 8 × 10 black-and-white photograph that has just
been slapped down on the desktop.*
    The picture is of ABBY *and* RAY *in bed together in the motel
room.*

VOICE: I know a place you can get that framed.

*The voice is familiar as that of the narrator whose musings on
life in Texas and the Soviet Union opened the movie.*
    We cut to him.
    He is settling himself into a chair facing the desk. He is
LOREN VISSER, *a large unshaven man in a misshapen yellow
leisure suit.*
    He smiles at the man behind the desk.

JULIAN MARTY

*sits staring down at the photograph. Behind him a window
opens on the bar proper. Country-western music filters in
from the bar.*
    MARTY *is not pleased.*

MARTY: What did you take these for?

VISSER: What do you mean . . .

Dan Hedaya (Marty)

He removes a pouch of tobacco from his breast pocket and nonchalantly starts rolling a cigarette.

. . . Just doin' my job.

MARTY: You called me, I knew they were there, so what do I need these for?

VISSER: Well, I don't know . . . Call it a fringe benefit.

MARTY: How long did you watch her?

VISSER: Most of the night . . .

He lights his cigarette, then slaps his lighter onto the desktop. It is silver, engraved on the top with a lariat spelling out "Loren" in script, and on the side with a declaration that he is "Elks Man of the Year."

. . . They'd just rest a few minutes and then get started again. Quite something.

MARTY stares down at the photograph.

MARTY: You know in Greece they cut off the head of the messenger who brought bad news.

A smoke ring floats into frame from offscreen.

VISSER: Now that don't make much sense.

MARTY: No. It just made them feel better.

MARTY rises and goes to a safe behind his desk.
VISSER laughs as he watches MARTY.

VISSER: Well first off, Julian, I don't know what the story is in Greece but in this state we got very definite laws about that . . .

MARTY, hunched over the standing safe behind his desk, tosses in the photograph and takes out a pay envelope.

. . . Second place I ain't a messenger, I'm a private investigator. And third place—and most important—it ain't such bad news. I mean you thought he was a colored (*he laughs*) . . . You're always assumin' the worst . . .

VISSER blows another smoke ring, pushes a fat finger through the middle of it, and beams at MARTY.

. . . Anything else?

MARTY: Yeah, don't come by here any more. If I need you again I know which rock to turn over.

MARTY *scales the pay envelope across the desk. It hits* VISSER
in the chest and bounces to the floor.

VISSER *looks stonily down at the envelope; no expression
for a beat. Then he roars with laughter.*

VISSER: That's good . . . "which rock to turn over"
. . . that's very good . . .

*Sighing, he leans forward to pick up the envelope. He rises,
straightens his cowboy hat, and walks over to a screen door
letting out on the bar's back parking lot.*

VISSER: Well, gimme a call whenever you wanna cut
off my head . . .

*He pauses at the door, cocks his head, then turns back to the
desk and picks up his cigarette lighter. Returning to the door:*

. . . I can crawl around without it.

The door slams shut behind him.
    MARTY *scowls at the back door. After a moment he rises
and crosses the office to the window looking out on the bar.*
    Over MARTY's *shoulder we see the long bar leading up to
the window in perpendicular. The camera is tracking
forward, past* MARTY, *to frame on the window.*
    *A black man is just now vaulting the near end of the bar,
over onto the customer side.*

MATCH CUT TO:
MARTY'S BAR
REVERSE ANGLE   VAULTING MAN

*Tracking back with him as he lands on the customer side and
heads across the bar. This shot, from the other side of the
back-office window, reveals the window to be a one-way glass
mirrored on this side.*
    MEURICE, *the black bartender, is muscular, about 200*

pounds, dressed in white pants and a sleeveless T-shirt. He is
making his way through the crowd toward the jukebox.
Another man stands in front of it examining the selections.
He deposits a quarter.

MEURICE: Hold it, hold it. What's tonight?

MAN: What?

MEURICE: What night is it?

MAN (*studying* MEURICE):   . . . Friday?

MEURICE: Right. Friday night is Yankee night. Where're
you from?

MAN: Lubbock?

MEURICE shakes his head and punches the selector buttons on
the jukebox.

MEURICE: Right. I'm from Detroit (*turning to leave*). It's
a big city up north with tall buildings.

A Motown song drops. We track behind MEURICE as he
makes his way back toward the bar. When he reaches it, he
claps a couple of people on the shoulder, who make way for
him. He vaults back over the top, walks down the bar, and
stops in front of an attractive white woman sitting on a bar
stool and sipping a brandy.

MEURICE: Where was I?

WOMAN: You were telling me about the Ring of Fire.

MEURICE: Yeah, well, I may be getting in over my head
here, I mean you're the geologist, but my theory for what

it's worth, you got all these volcanoes and each time each one pops it's the equivalent of what, twenty, thirty megatons of TNT? enough to light Vegas for how long? how many years? Course, I'm no mathematician but—

MARTY:　　Meurice.

MARTY is approaching from the direction of the office.

MEURICE:　　Yeah, I know. Pour 'em short.

MARTY:　　Has Ray come in yet?

MEURICE:　　No, he's off tonight. Where was he last night?

MARTY (*glaring*):　　How would I know?

MEURICE:　　I don't know, didn't he call?

MARTY loses his glare and his gaze drifts over to the woman. After an awkward pause, MEURICE clears his throat.

. . . Marty, I'd like you to meet an old friend of mine, Debra. Debra, this is Julian Marty, the dude I'm always talking about.

She is unselfconsciously returning MARTY's stare.

MARTY:　　If he does come in I'm not here . . . What were you drinking, Debra?

DEBRA:　　Remy.

MARTY:　　You've got a very sophisticated palate.

DEBRA:　　Thanks.

MARTY: Give Debra here another drink, and give me the usual.

MEURICE walks down the bar.

DEBRA: . . . What's a palate?

MARTY studies her for a beat, she studies him, he smiles.

MARTY: Listen, I got tickets for the Oilers and the Rams next week in the Astrodome. Ever sat on the fifty yard line?

DEBRA: I don't follow baseball.

MARTY laughs.

MARTY: You won't have to. I'll explain what a palate is.

DEBRA: You won't have to. I just wanted to see if you knew.

MARTY smiles bleakly. DEBRA drains her glass as MEURICE returns. He sets another Cognac in front of DEBRA, and a glass of milk in front of Marty.

MARTY: What's this?

MEURICE: You said the usual—

MARTY: Red Label.

MEURICE (*picking up the milk*):   Right. Sorry.

MARTY: Pour that back.

MEURICE: What.

MARTY: Don't throw that out.

MEURICE: Right.

He wanders on down the bar; MARTY's attention returns to the woman.

MARTY: So how long have you known Meurice?

DEBRA: About ten years.

MARTY's attention is caught by something down the bar. He half-rises from his stool.

MARTY: What—Waitaminute—What . . .

HIS POV

MEURICE is pouring the milk down the sink. He looks innocently up.

MEURICE: What.

BACK TO MARTY

Angry but not knowing what to say. He glances around the bar, sinks slowly back onto his stool.

MARTY: Deuce in the corner needs help.

MEURICE: Right.

MARTY sits staring across the bar for a moment, nods a couple of times at nothing in particular, then looks back at the woman.

MARTY: . . . So what're you doing tonight?

DEBRA: Going out with Meurice.

MARTY tosses a beer nut into his mouth.

MARTY: Tell him you have a headache.

DEBRA gives him a level stare.

DEBRA: It'll pass.

MARTY: We don't seem to be communicating—

DEBRA: You want to hustle me. I don't want to be
hustled. It's as simple as that. Now that I've
communicated, why don't you leave?

MARTY: I own the place.

DEBRA: Christ, I'm getting bored.

MARTY: I'm not surprised, the company you've been
keeping the last ten years.

*They both fall silent as MEURICE enters frame. He takes a
bottle from the bar and pours himself a drink.*

MARTY: What's this?

MEURICE: What.

MARTY (*pointing at MEURICE's drink*):   This.

MEURICE: Jack Daniels. Don't worry, I'm paying for it.

MARTY: That's not the point.

MEURICE: What's the point?

MARTY: The point is we don't serve niggers here.

MEURICE: Where? (*He looks over his shoulder; up and down the bar*) . . . I'm very careful about that.

MARTY tosses back MEURICE's drink, then turns to DEBRA, smiling.

MARTY: He thinks I'm kidding. Everybody thinks I'm kidding; (*as he turns to leave*) if Ray comes in I'm not home.

DEBRA watches him go, then turns back to MEURICE.

DEBRA: Nice guy.

MEURICE: Not really. What'd you say your last name was?

MARTY'S HOUSE   TRACKING DOWN HALLWAY

We are following a large German shepherd as it pads down the hall toward a warmly lit room at its end. We hear only the sound of the dog's paws on the hardwood floor, and the faint clicking of billiard balls.

BILLIARD ROOM

It is a paneled, carpeted room with black leather furniture and a nine-foot billiard table. Various stuffed animal trophies are scattered around the room, including a moose head mounted on one wall. RAY stands alone in the foreground, shooting pool, an unlit cigarette in his mouth. The room is very quiet.
  In the background the German shepherd enters from the hallway, sits down in a corner, and benignly watches RAY.

UPSTAIRS BEDROOM

It is expensively appointed; a brightly lit woman's bedroom. ABBY is opening a hinged drawer in a white antique bureau. She pulls out a leather handbag, gropes nervously through its contents, then puts it aside.

She crosses the room to a vanity table, takes a purse from underneath, and spills its contents out on top of the table.

BILLIARD ROOM

RAY *pockets a couple of balls, looks over at the dog, then up at the wall at the far end of the room.*

RAY'S POV

Hanging on the wall are a couple of framed photographs of MARTY *and* ABBY, *taken a long time ago.*

BACK TO RAY

Staring at the pictures. He looks back down at the pool table.

UPSTAIRS BEDROOM

ABBY *is sitting on a large double bed. She puts aside another purse, rises and crosses the room hurriedly, and pushes back the sliding doors of a long wardrobe closet. The upper shelf is lined with handbags—fifteen or twenty of them. She grabs the first one, looks in, tosses it aside; grabs the second, looks—and stops.*

HER POV

Inside the purse, a small pearl-handled gun.

BILLIARD ROOM

RAY *is now standing in front of the pictures on the wall, looking from one to the next.*

RAY'S POV

A picture of ABBY *and* MARTY *standing together on a Gulf beach.* MARTY *is wearing a long velour beach robe,* ABBY *is in a swimming suit.* RAY's *hand enters frame. He traces a finger down her leg.*

CLOSE SHOT   RAY

His head cocked to the side. After a moment his eyes shift.

EXTREME CLOSE SHOT   PHOTO DETAIL

Of MARTY's face. He is staring into the camera, at whoever took the picture. His head is thrown back slightly; he is laughing.

From offscreen in the quiet room we hear a static hum and then ABBY's voice over an intercom.

ABBY'S VOICE: Ray. . . ?

BACK TO RAY

He turns from the photograph and walks to an intercom speaker next to the mounted moose's head. He presses the speaker button.

RAY: Yeah . . .

He idly takes his unlit cigarette and sticks it in the moose's mouth.

. . . You get what you wanted?

ABBY'S VOICE: Yeah. Let's get out of here.

MARTY'S FRONT FOYER

We are looking across a dark, high-ceilinged foyer toward the front door. RAY leans against the doorjamb, in silhouette in the open doorway. He is facing a curved staircase that descends into the foyer. ABBY appears at the second-floor landing and starts down the stairs.

RAY: Why d'you wanna leave all this?

ABBY: You kidding? I don't wanna leave all this, I just wanna leave Marty . . .

As she reaches the bottom of the stairs:

  . . . Drive me to a motel?

RAY: You can stay at my place, I'll drop you there.

ABBY: Where . . . where you going?

RAY: See a guy.

ABBY (*nervously*):   Don't go to the bar, Ray. I know him, that ain't a good idea.

RAY: I just gotta see a guy.

MARTY'S BAR

The crowd has thinned out. MEURICE and DEBRA are in the foreground.
    RAY enters from the street and makes his way over to them.

MEURICE: Howdy stranger.

RAY: Meurice. Sorry I didn't show last night.

MEURICE: Wasn't too busy. You missed a good one, though. This white guy walks in about one o'clock, asks if we have a discount for alcoholics . . .
    I tell him to get lost, but Marty's sitting here listening and I can tell he's thinking that maybe it ain't such a bad idea . . .

He pours DEBRA another drink and starts to set one up for RAY.

. . . Ray, this is Debra. She's a geologist. That's the theory of rocks.

RAY nods at DEBRA.

RAY: Is Marty here?

MEURICE: Not here tonight. Wasn't here last night. He's especially not back in his office.

RAY (*leaving*):   Thanks Meurice.

MEURICE: For what?

EXT   BACK OF MARTY'S BAR

MARTY is sitting on the stoop that descends from his back office to a graveled back parking lot; he is framed in the open doorway of his brightly lit office. He stares fixedly at something offscreen.

MARTY'S POV

In the middle distance a huge incinerator operates full blast. Orange flames lick out the sides; white smoke billows out the top. Two figures in silhouette are chucking garbage in through a large gate.

BACK TO MARTY

Behind him, in the office, we see the door from the bar open, and RAY entering.

RAY: Marty?

MARTY looks over his shoulder, then back toward the furnace. RAY descends the stoop and stands in front of him.

. . . Well. . . ? What?

MARTY stares past RAY across the parking lot.

MARTY: What "what"?

RAY: Am I fired? You wanna hit me? What?

MARTY: I don't particularly want to talk to you.

RAY: Well . . . if you're not gonna fire me I might as well quit.

MARTY: Fine. Suit yourself (*still staring fixedly at the furnace*) . . . Having a good time?

RAY tenses. There is a pause.

RAY: . . . I don't like this kind of talk.

MARTY still stares at the furnace.

MARTY: Then what'd you come here for?

RAY (*no more conciliation*):   You owe me for two weeks.

MARTY shakes his head.

MARTY: Nope. She's an expensive piece of ass . . .

He finally looks up at RAY.

. . . You get a refund though, if you tell me who else she's been sluicing.

RAY: I want that money. If you wanna tell me something, fine—

MARTY: What're you, a fucking marriage counselor?

RAY breaks into a strained half-smile.
   MARTY grins humorlessly back, mimicking RAY's smile.

MARTY: What're you smiling at—I'm a funny guy,
right, I'm an asshole? No no, that's not what's funny.
What's funny is her. What's funny is that I had you two
followed because, if it isn't you, she's been sleeping with
someone else . . .

*He grabs a knee in each hand and leans forward, still looking
at RAY. He is becoming only slightly more animated.*

. . . What's really going to be funny is when she gives
you that innocent look and says, What're you talking
about, Ray, I haven't done anything funny . . .

He leans back again.

. . . But the funniest thing to me right now is that you
think she came back here for you—*that's* what's funny.

*RAY moves forward and MARTY's eyes follow him as he
approaches. MARTY's smile abruptly turns to a look of
apprehension. RAY enters frame and brushes past MARTY as
he walks up the stoop, and crosses the back office toward the
bar.*
   MARTY relaxes, and his gaze returns to the furnace.

. . . Come on this property again and I'll be forced to
shoot you . . .

RAY opens the door to the bar and shuts it softly behind him.

. . . Fair notice.

MARTY'S OFFICE   LATER
CLOSE SHOT   CEILING FAN

At the cut the music and all other bar noise drops out. We hear only the rhythmic whir of the fan. We tilt down from the ceiling fan to frame MARTY, *tilted back in his desk chair, staring up at the fan.*

MEURICE (*os*):   Marty . . .

WIDE SHOT   THE OFFICE

MEURICE *is standing in the door to the bar. Far behind him we can see* DEBRA *waiting in the dimly lit, deserted bar.*

MEURICE: . . . I thought you were dead. Going home?

MARTY: No. I think I'll stay right here in hell.

MEURICE (*turning to leave*):   Kind of a bleak point of view there, isn't it Marty?

MARTY: Meurice . . .

MEURICE *pauses in the doorway.*

. . . I don't want that asshole near my money. I don't even want him in the bar.

MEURICE: We get a lot of assholes in here, Marty.

MEURICE *and* DEBRA *can be heard leaving the bar.* MARTY *looks down at the telephone in front of him on the desk, then picks up the receiver and dials. He tilts back in his chair and stares back up at the ceiling.*

MARTY'S POV

The ceiling fan, turning slowly.

EXT   RAY'S BUNGALOW FROM INSIDE RAY'S CAR

In the foreground RAY *sits behind the wheel of his parked car, slumped back against the seat. He is staring at his one-story bungalow, in which a couple of lights are burning. Inside we can faintly hear his telephone ringing.*
It rings for a long time.

RAY'S LIVING ROOM
CLOSE SHOT   THE RINGING TELEPHONE

ABBY's *hand enters frame, hesitates, then after another ring picks up.*

ABBY: Hello?

There is no answer. From the other end we hear only the rhythmic whir of a ceiling fan.

MARTY'S OFFICE

MARTY *listens. He says nothing, still tilted back in his chair, staring at the ceiling.*

RAY'S LIVING ROOM

ABBY *listens. She shifts the phone to her other ear, listening hard to the sound of the fan. There is another long pause.*

ABBY: . . . Marty?

The phone goes dead just as we hear the front door opening.
ABBY *looks up as she cradles the phone.*
RAY *is standing in the doorway.*

RAY: Who was it?

ABBY: What?

RAY: On the phone. Was it for you?

Frances McDormand (Abby)

ABBY: I don't know, he didn't say anything.

RAY: Uh-huh. So how do you know it was a he?

ABBY (*smiling*):   You got a girl—am I screwing something up by being here?

RAY *leans against the door and folds his arms, watching* ABBY.

RAY: No, am I?

ABBY *looks at him, puzzled. After an uncomfortable pause:*

ABBY: . . . I can find a place tomorrow, then I'll be outta your hair.

RAY: If that's what you want to do, then you oughta do it. You, uh . . . you want the bed or the couch?

ABBY shifts uneasily, looking at RAY.

ABBY: Well . . . the couch would be all right . . .

RAY: You can sleep on the bed if you want.

ABBY: Well . . . I'm not gonna put you out of your bed . . .

RAY: You wouldn't be putting me out.

ABBY: . . . Well, I'd be okay in here—

RAY walks toward the bedroom.

RAY: Okay.

MARTY'S OFFICE   LATER

Still tilted back in his chair, MARTY stares glumly at the ceiling. The bar itself is completely still except for the rhythmic whir of the fan.

CLOSE SHOT   A CEILING FAN

Turning slowly. We tilt down from the fan to frame ABBY, lying under a sheet on RAY's couch, staring up at the fan in the darkened living room. The room is still. We hear only the whir of the fan and the distant sound of crickets. ABBY turns her head, looking offscreen.

HER POV

A ray of light slants up the hallway from the direction of the bedroom. The light is snapped off, leaving the hallway in darkness. We hear a faint cough and the creaking of bedsprings.

RAY'S BEDROOM

RAY lies in bed, staring at the ceiling.

RAY'S LIVING ROOM/HALLWAY
LONG SHOT   THE LIVING ROOM   FROM THE HALLWAY

ABBY sits up. She stands and walks across the moonlit room toward the hallway. We pull her back down the hall toward the bedroom. She pauses in the bedroom doorway and looks down toward the bed.

ABBY'S POV

RAY in bed, his eyes closed.

BACK TO ABBY

We pull her as she enters the room, then tilt down with her as she hesitantly sits on the edge of the bed.

ABBY'S POV

Close shot, RAY asleep.

BACK TO ABBY

Framed against a moonlit window from the shoulders up.
    There is a long pause.
    RAY's hand enters frame and pulls ABBY down out of frame onto the bed. We hold on the moonlit window.

DISSOLVE THROUGH TO:
SAME WINDOW   SAME ANGLE   PRE-DAWN

Through the window the slow dissolve gradually defines the front lawn and the street beyond in the flat pre-dawn light. ABBY rises into frame and quietly gets out of bed. The camera tracks behind her as she walks up the hallway into the living room.
    We follow her across the living room and move into a close

shot on her hand as she reaches into her purse and withdraws a small plastic compact.

LOW-ANGLE CLOSE SHOT   ABBY

She flips open the compact, then, hearing something, looks up, squinting across the room.

ABBY'S POV

In the shadows at the far end of the room we can just see two pointed ears and a glittering pair of eyes. The German shepherd is panting softly.

OVER ABBY'S SHOULDER

As she peers into the shadows, her face reflected in the mirror of the open compact.

ABBY: Opal—

In the mirror something moves just behind her. ABBY starts to turn.
  MARTY's hand clamps over her mouth from behind. His other hand circles her waist. ABBY struggles.

MARTY (*quietly*):   Lover-boy oughta lock his door . . .

MARTY's hand drops from her waist to her thighs and slides under the robe.

. . . Lotta nuts out there.

Still holding her from behind, MARTY forces her down on her knees. ABBY's cries are muffled by the hand clamped over her mouth. MARTY shoots a glance down the dark hallway. There is no movement.
  ABBY's hand is groping forward out of frame.

CLOSE SHOT   ABBY'S PURSE

She upsets it. The contents spill out, among them a small pearl-handled revolver. Her hand gropes for the gun.

BACK TO ABBY AND MARTY

MARTY *yanks her to her feet, looking down the hallway.*

MARTY: Let's do it outside . . .

He is dragging her to the front door.

. . . in nature.

He pushes her through the screen door.

EXT   RAY'S BUNGALOW

The neighborhood is deserted and still. The streetlamps are still on. MARTY *and* ABBY *stumble down the front stoop onto the lawn.*

His hand is still clamped over her mouth. She reaches up, grabs a finger, and bends it back.

We hear the bone snap.

MARTY *screams. His hand drops. His other hand cuffs her on the side of the head, spinning her around.*

MARTY *is now clutching his broken finger with his good hand.* ABBY *kicks him in the groin.*

He sinks to his knees, drops forward on one hand, and vomits.

FRONT STOOP

RAY *is coming out the door, hitching up his pants. In his right hand he holds* ABBY's *pearl-handled revolver.*

MARTY

Slowly gets to his feet, looking at RAY.

ABBY

She has backed away from MARTY *and now stands on the lawn, breathing heavily. She looks from* RAY *to* MARTY.

BACK TO MARTY

Backing toward his car, a Cadillac parked at curbside, still looking at RAY. *He turns to get into the car.*

The German shepherd lopes across the lawn and takes a clean leap into the car through the open window on the passenger side.

MARTY *turns the ignition. The engine coughs and dies. He tries again; it starts.*

The car roars up the street.

RAY

Watching the car. He looks at ABBY.

ABBY

Still panting. Up the street we can hear MARTY's *car braking and grinding gears.*

RAY *enters to embrace* ABBY. *We hear* MARTY's *car alternately racing and stopping, shifting in and out of gear. His engine rumble starts to grow louder again.*

RAY: Like to have seen his face when he found the dead end.

In the background we see MARTY's *car roar by in the opposite direction.*

MOUNT BONNEL.   EVENING
LATERAL TRACK

Moving past a row of cars parked on an overlook near the top of the mountain. Below we can see the lights of the city of Austin. The lot is littered with beer cans. We hear the sound of rock music coming from various car radios. Several teenagers lean against cars drinking beer; inside the cars we can see the vague forms of others.

TEENAGER: Hey mister, how'd you break your pussy-finger?

His friends laugh.

TRACK PULLING MARTY

Ignoring the laughter as he walks past the cars, apparently looking for someone. His right index finger is taped up in an aluminum splint.

MARTY'S POV

At the end of a row of cars we see a green Volkswagen bug. Leaning against the hood is VISSER, *still dressed in his rumpled yellow suit. He is smoking a cigarette, talking to a sixteen-year-old girl in shorts and a tube top. When he notices* MARTY:

VISSER (*to the girl*):   Sorry sweetheart, my date is here . . .

The girl drifts off. MARTY *enters frame and* VISSER *turns to him.*

. . . She saw me rolling a cigarette and thought it was marijuana (*he laughs*). I guess she thought I was a swinger.

VISSER opens the back door of the car. MARTY *ignores the invitation, walks around to the front door on the passenger side and gets in.*

INT VISSER'S CAR

As VISSER *gets into the driver's seat. A small topless doll is suspended from the rearview mirror.* VISSER *gives it a tap. As it swings back and forth two small lights, one behind each breast, blink on and off.*

VISSER: Idnat wild?

Both men sit watching the doll intently.
    Finally MARTY *reaches up and stops its swinging with the rounded end of his splint.* VISSER *eyes the splint.*

VISSER (*genially*):   Stick your finger up the wrong person's ass?

MARTY *is silent, but* VISSER *is in a good mood.*

VISSER: You know a friend of mine broke his hand a while back. Put in a cast. Very next day he takes a fall, protects his bad hand, falls on his good one, breaks that too. So now he's got two busted flippers and I say to him "Creighton, I hope your wife loves you. 'Cause for the next five weeks you cannot wipe your own goddamn ass . . ."

Overcome by laughter. Finally:

. . . That's the test, ain't it? Test of true love—

MARTY: Got a job for you.

VISSER (*settling down*):   . . . Well, if the pay's right and it's legal I'll do it.

MARTY: It's not strictly legal.

VISSER shrugs, lights up another cigarette with his fraternally inscribed lighter and drops the lighter onto the dashboard.

VISSER: If the pay's right I'll do it.

MARTY: It's, uh . . . it's in reference to that gentleman and my wife. The more I think about it the more irritated I get.

VISSER: Yeah? Well how irritated are you?

MARTY doesn't answer. Finally VISSER laughs.

. . . Gee, I'm sorry to hear that. Can you tell me what you want me to do or is it a secret?

MARTY: Listen, I'm not—this isn't a joke here.

VISSER eyes him, still smiling. Finally he shrugs.

VISSER: You want me to kill 'em.

MARTY: I didn't say that (*a pause*). . . . Well?

VISSER: Well what?

MARTY: What do you think?

VISSER: You're an idiot.

MARTY's shoulders slump. He seems less tense, almost relieved.

MARTY: So, uh . . . this wouldn't interest you.

VISSER: I didn't say that. All I said was you're an idiot. Hell, you been thinking about it so much it's driving you simple.

They are staring at each other.

MARTY: Ten thousand dollars I'll give you.

VISSER laughs again.

VISSER: I'm supposed to do a murder—two murders— and just trust you not to go simple on me and do something stupid. I mean real stupid. Now why should I trust you?

MARTY: For the money.

VISSER (*sobering*): The money. Yeah. That's a right smart of money . . .

He turns and gazes out the window.

. . . In Russia they make only fifty cent a day.

He falls silent again, still staring out the window.
In the closeness of the car MARTY is starting to sweat.

MARTY (*hoarsely*): . . . There's a big—

VISSER (*abruptly*): I want you to go fishing.

MARTY: . . . What?

VISSER: Go down to Corpus for a few days. Get yourself noticed. I'll give you a call when it's done . . . You just find a way to cover that money.

MARTY *is slumped in his seat, not responding to the fact that* VISSER *has just ended the conversation.*

   Finally he rouses himself and gets out of the car, leaving VISSER *staring at the door he has left open behind him.*

   After a moment we hear MARTY's *footsteps approaching again, and he leans back into the open door with an afterthought.*

MARTY: I'll take care of the money, you just make sure those bodies aren't found . . . There's a . . .

These words are difficult to say.

   . . . If you want, there's a big incinerator behind my place . . .

The two men look at each other. MARTY *leaves. After a moment,* VISSER *leans over to grab the handle of the still open door.*

VISSER (*under his breath*):   Sweet Jesus, you are disgusting.

The door slams.

INT EMPTY APARTMENT NIGHT

The apartment is dark. We are looking across a shadowy floor towards a large window, through which cold blue street light shines. Through the window we can see the facade of the building across the street; we are three or four floors up.

   We can hear the animated, accented voice of an Hispanic woman approaching the apartment from the hallway behind us.

LANDLADY (*os*):   —big windows, paneleen and everytheen. So you want, like your own place? Like a Town House?

A crack of light shoots across the floor as we hear the apartment door open behind us. A figure enters frame. As it crosses into the shaft of light we see that it is ABBY. She moves across the dark apartment, in silhouette against the window.

LANDLADY (*os*):   No one will bother you here, sweetie—

An overhead light is switched on and the room is bathed in light. Several feet from ABBY, an old man in a dirty undershirt is asleep on a cot. ABBY starts.
     The old man grumbles, slowly sits up, squints.
     With the light, the window behind ABBY has become a mirror of the entire room, in which we now see the matronly LANDLADY standing by the wall switch.
     The LANDLADY roars at the old man in Spanish. The man glowers at her. The LANDLADY looks back at ABBY.

LANDLADY (*cheerful again*):   I show you around.

We follow ABBY as she accompanies the landlady back into the short hallway–entrance foyer. ABBY glances back at the old man.

ABBY: Are you sure this is . . . Are you sure this apartment is vacant? . . . Mrs. Esteves?

The LANDLADY laughs cheerfully.

LANDLADY: Oh yes . . .

She gestures to a kitchen alcove on the left.

. . . That's the kitchen . . .

She turns and throws a few more barbs in Spanish back toward the old man, then opens a door on the right side of the foyer and enters the bathroom.

. . . This is the bathroom . . .

She flushes the toilet.

. . . The toilet works and everytheen . . .

She bustles out of the bathroom and takes the two short steps back into the main room. She gestures expansively.

. . . And here we are back in the liveen room.

She gives one vigorous stomp.

. . . Good floors. Gas heat.

She points.

. . . That's Mr. Garcia.

The old man is now sitting on the edge of the bed, smoking a cigarette, looking for a place to put the ash. The LANDLADY *snaps at him again in Spanish, and is again cheerful as she turns back to address* ABBY.

. . . I was just esplaineen to him that he moved out of here yesterday . . .

She walks toward the apartment door.

. . . You look around. Don't mind Mr. Garcia; he use do be my brother-in-law.

She walks out and shuts the door.
  The room is quiet.

CLOSE SHOT   ABBY

Staring at the door. She looks at MR. GARCIA, *looks nervously around the apartment. She looks back at* MR. GARCIA.

CLOSE SHOT   MR. GARCIA

Staring vacantly at ABBY. *He blows a stream of smoke across
the room. The ash falls off his cigarette.*

**STRIP BAR   NIGHT
EXHORTER'S CUBICLE**

*Hunched over the public address microphone in his small
cubicle of exhortation, is the middle-aged strip-bar barker.
Years of service in the bar have left his exhortations
depressingly bereft of conviction.*

EXHORTER: How 'bout it, gentlemen, let's show our
appreciation for Lorraine up there, a registered nurse
from Bolton, Texas, how 'bout it gentlemen, yeah . . .

THE BAR PROPER

MEURICE *is one of a line of men sitting at the bar, all looking
intently at the same point off left. All of the men except*
MEURICE *are conservatively dressed and apparently well-to-
do. An audio loop is blaring a bump-and-grind version of
"Yellow Rose of Texas," punctuated by the crash of cymbals
and the thumping of toms.*
    ABBY *enters and sits into an empty chair next to* MEURICE.

ABBY: Looks like the state legislature is out of session.

MEURICE *continues to stare intently off.*

MEURICE: I thought this was where they met.

All of the heads at the bar start to swivel, including
MEURICE'S. *A couple of patrons hurriedly snatch their drinks
off the bar.*
    *In the extreme foreground a stripper dances on top of the
bar into frame. We crop her just above her white high-heeled
cowboy boots and her bare calves.*

Frances McDormand, seated at far left, and Samm-Art Williams (Meurice), second from left

The conversation continues with ABBY *looking at* MEURICE, *but* MEURICE *and everyone else at the bar looking up at a point somewhere above the stripper's bare calves.*

ABBY: Listen Meurice, you're gonna help me with a problem.

MEURICE: I am?

The stripper drops a white leatherette vest onto the bar in the foreground. The audience cheers.

ABBY: You're gonna keep an eye on Marty and Ray, make sure nothing happens.

MEURICE: It won't?

Two sheriff-star pasties drop onto the bar. The audience cheers.

. . . Ever occur to you, Abby, that maybe I'm the wrong person to ask?

THE EXHORTER

Into his microphone.

EXHORTER: Let's not sit on our wallets, gentlemen. Lorraine is up there dancing her heart out, and if you let that cash money set on your hip, you might just as well be broke . . .

ABBY AND MEURICE

She is rising to leave; he is still staring off.

ABBY: Thanks, Meurice.

MEURICE: Any time. But you don't have to worry about a thing for a while. Marty went down to Corpus yesterday.

An old-west gunbelt hits the bar. The audience roars.

THE EXHORTER

Into his microphone.

EXHORTER: And remember, gentlemen, we're always here, two to two, A.M. to P.M., three hundred and sixty-four days and Christmas, God willing and the creek don't rise . . .

RAY'S BEDROOM

The room is dark. We are looking across the room toward a moonlit window. Beyond, across the lawn, the lamplit street is empty.
Suddenly ABBY sits bolt upright into frame from the bed below.

ABBY: He's in the house.

Offscreen we hear RAY *stirring in bed.*

RAY: What's the matter?

ABBY twists around to look down at him.

ABBY: I could've sworn I heard something.

RAY: Door's locked. Nothing there.

He pulls her down out of frame and we hold on the window and the empty lamplit street. Then ABBY *rises back into frame, in silhouette against the window, looking down at* RAY.

ABBY: I knew it. 'Cause we wouldn't have heard anything if it was him. He's real careful. Fact is, he's anal.

RAY: . . . Huh?

ABBY: Yeah, he told me once himself. He said to me . . .

She taps herself on the forehead.

. . . "In here, Abby. In here . . . I'm anal."

HIGH ANGLE   RAY

Looking up at Abby.

RAY (*yawning*):   . . . Well I'll be damned.

ABBY: I couldn't believe it either . . .

SIDE ANGLE   ABBY

Framed against the window, looking down at RAY.

ABBY: . . . Me on the other hand, I got lots of personality . . .

She drops down onto the bed out of frame. The camera holds on the window through which we see the empty lamplit street.

ABBY: Marty always said I had too much. 'Course he was never big on personality . . .

She rises back up into frame, in silhouette against the window.

. . . He sent me to a psychiatrist to see if he could calm me down some.

RAY: Yeah? What happened?

ABBY: Psychiatrist said I was the healthiest person he'd ever met, so Marty fired him.

RAY (*sleepily*):   . . . I don't know if you can fire a psychiatrist, exactly.

ABBY: Well, I didn't see him anymore, I'll tell you that much.

HIGH ANGLE   RAY

His eyes half-closed.

RAY: Uh-huh.

ABBY: I said, Marty, how come *you're* anal and *I* gotta go to the psychiatrist?

RAY: What'd he say?

SIDE ANGLE   ABBY

Framed against the window.

ABBY: Nothing. He's like you, he doesn't say much.

RAY (*murmuring*):   Thanks.

ABBY: Except when he doesn't say things they're usually nasty.

RAY: . . . Mm-hmm.

ABBY: When you don't they're usually nice.

RAY: . . . You ever get tired?

ABBY: Huh? Oh, yeah, I guess. Mm-hmm.

RAY's hand rises into frame and coaxes ABBY back down onto the bed, revealing, through the window, a green Volkswagen now parked at curbside on the lamplit street.
  We hear the rustle of sheets.
  As we hold on the window, we begin to hear the faint, distant sound of metal scraping against metal.

HALLWAY/LIVING ROOM

We track down the dark hallway into the living room. As the camera advances the sound of the scraping becomes louder.
  We are moving across the living room up to the front door of the bungalow. The scraping is louder still as we finally frame on a close shot of the doorknob, which is jiggling ever so slightly.

We hear a click as the lock finally releases.

The door swings slowly open, revealing a man's hand on the outside doorknob. We follow the hand as the man advances slowly and quietly across the living room.

ABBY's *purse comes into frame, sitting on a bureau; next to it is a large tote bag. The hand rummages through the tote bag briefly, then the purse. The man withdraws* ABBY's *pearl-handled revolver. He breaks it open.*

LOW-ANGLE CLOSE SHOT   THE MAN'S FACE

It is VISSER. *As we hear a click offscreen, his face glows a dim orange.*

BACK TO HIS HANDS

His right holds the revolver, cylinder open, inside the purse. His left holds his cigarette lighter as he inspects the chamber. Three of the holes glint silver, the other three are black—empty.

We hear the faint creaking of bedsprings.

WIDE SHOT   LIVING ROOM

VISSER *cocks his head, listening, and looks down the hallway. He takes a couple of quiet steps across the living room and, as the camera tracks up to him, opens the back door of the bungalow.*

We follow him outside onto the lawn.

EXT   RAY'S BUNGALOW

We track behind him as he rounds the corner of the house and approaches the open window to RAY's *bedroom. He slows, moves more cautiously, then sinks to his knees under the window. As he reaches into his breast pocket the camera continues tracking up to and over him, finally framing his POV through the window.*

On the bed inside we can dimly see ABBY *and* RAY, *asleep.*

We have been hearing a faint rumble, becoming louder and

louder as if approaching from a distance. Just as the rumble becomes deafening a sudden bright flash of light illuminates the room, seeming to polarize the image of ABBY *and* RAY *in bed, and we:*

CUT TO:
EXT   PHONE BOOTH   DAY

A huge truck roars by on the street behind VISSER, *and with it the deafening rumble recedes. It is a painfully bright day.* VISSER *stands sweating in the phone booth with the receiver pressed to his ear. We hear the phone ringing at the other end.*

   Finally, it is picked up.

VOICE: Hello.

VISSER: Marty?

MARTY: Yeah. Is it . . .

VISSER: Ya catch any fish?

M. Emmet Walsh (Visser)

MARTY: . . . What?

VISSER: Ya catch any fish?

MARTY: Yeah . . .

VISSER: . . . What kind of fish?

MARTY: Listen, what is it? Is it done?

VISSER forces a chuckle.

VISSER: . . . Yessir, you owe me some money.

MARTY'S OFFICE   NIGHT
CLOSE SHOT   TWO STRINGS OF FISH

Being plopped down onto MARTY's desk.

WIDER   THE OFFICE

*VISSER sits facing the desk. He lights himself a cigarette and
sets the lighter down on the desk in front of him. MARTY
settles, fidgeting, into the chair behind it.*
    *The bar is quiet, shut down. We hear only the whir of a fan
somewhere offscreen. MARTY and VISSER are lit by a lamp on
the desk between them. Light streams into the room from a
bathroom in the background. VISSER is looking at the dead
fish.*

VISSER (*dully*):   They look good.

*MARTY half-rises from his seat and picks up one of the
strings.*

MARTY: Want a couple?

*He drops them on VISSER's side of the desk. VISSER's head
draws back: he was only being polite.*

VISSER: Just the ten thousand'll be fine.

MARTY: Got something to show me first?

VISSER hands a 9 × 12 envelope across the desk. MARTY stares at it for a moment, then quickly bends back the flap and takes out an 8 × 10 photograph.

THE PHOTOGRAPH

It is a black-and-white shot of ABBY and RAY in RAY's bed. The sheet that partially covers them is pocked with three dark bullet holes and is stained with blood.

MARTY

Staring dully down at the picture.

MARTY: Dead, huh?

VISSER: So it would seem.

CLOSE SHOT   THE TOP OF THE DESK

VISSER is pushing the fish away from his side of the desk with the eraser end of a pencil.

MARTY: What did you . . .

BACK TO MARTY

Still looking at the picture. He traces the outline of ABBY's body with his finger.

MARTY: . . . What did you do with the bodies?

VISSER: It's taken care of. The less you know about it the better.

MARTY: Jesus, I don't believe it . . .

MARTY *slips the picture back into its 9 × 12 envelope. His face is pale.*

MARTY: . . . I think I'm gonna be sick.

He rises and heads for the bathroom, still clutching the envelope.

CLOSE SHOT   VISSER

As his eyes follow MARTY's *exit. The bathroom door doesn't close all the way: a narrow shaft of light slices the office from the bare bulb in the bathroom.*

VISSER: I'll want that picture back . . .

He turns to look across the desk.

VISSER'S POV

The standing safe behind the desk.

BACK TO VISSER

Still looking at the safe. Beads of sweat have popped out on his forehead. He fans himself with his cowboy hat.

VISSER: . . . and you did say somethin' about some money.

We hear a toilet flush offscreen.

LONG SHOT   MARTY

As he reenters the office.

MARTY: Your money, yeah.

VISSER *stares dully down at the desktop.*

VISSER: Something I got to ask you, Marty. I been very very careful. Have you been very very careful?

MARTY: Of course.

VISSER: Nobody knows you hired me?

HIGH ANGLE   CORNER OF THE OFFICE

*MARTY is hunched over the open safe, still holding the
envelope. Blocking VISSER's view of the safe with his body, he
slides the picture of ABBY's and RAY's corpses from under the
envelope into the safe, then withdraws two packets of money.*

MARTY: Don't be absurd, I wasn't about to tell
anyone . . .

He shuts the safe and spins the dial.

. . . This is an illicit romance—we've got to trust each
other to be discreet . . .

*He walks across the room and throws the money and the
envelope down on the desk.*

. . . For richer, for poorer.

*VISSER looks from the money down at his hands. They are
sweating.*

VISSER: Don't say that. Your marriages don't work out
so hot . . .

He wipes his hands on his pants.

. . . How did you cover the money?

MARTY sits and props his booted feet up on the desk.

MARTY: It's taken care of. The less you know about it
the better.

He smiles.

. . . I just made a call about that. It'll look fine.

VISSER (*shaking his head*):   I must've gone money simple. This kind of murder . . .

He nods toward the envelope on the desk.

. . . it's too damn risky.

MARTY: Then you shouldn't have done it. Can't have it both ways.

He pushes the money across the desk with his boot.

. . . Count it if you want.

VISSER (*reaching into his coat*):   Nah, I trust ya.

His hand comes out with a gun pointing at MARTY *and—BAM—he fires, an orange lick of flame spurting from the gun.*
Both men sit frozen. VISSER's *hand is the only thing that moved.*

CLOSE SHOT   MARTY
Staring at VISSER.
After the gun blast we hear only the whir of the fan.

CLOSE SHOT   VISSER
Staring at MARTY.

MED SHOT   MARTY   OVER VISSER'S SHOULDER
His eyes are now shut. Otherwise he hasn't moved. A blood stain is growing on the front of his shirt.

WIDE SHOT   THE OFFICE

The two face each other across the desk. VISSER's gun is still trained on MARTY.

After a moment VISSER starts fanning himself again with his cowboy hat. The only movement in the frame is the slow back-and-forth of the yellow hat, rhythmically in and out of shadow as it catches and loses the light from the desk lamp. There is a long pause.

Finally one of MARTY's feet slips from the desk and hits the floor with a THUD.

VISSER lays the gun on the desk.

CLOSE SHOT   VISSER

As he reaches into his breast pocket and withdraws a handkerchief. He wipes his forehead, then picks up the gun and wipes it off. He leans down with the gun.

CLOSE SHOT   THE GUN

As VISSER places it deliberately on the floor near the desk. It is ABBY's pearl-handled revolver.

THE DESKTOP   FROM DESK LEVEL

As VISSER straightens up in the foreground. From our head-on angle shooting across the desk we can see the bright metallic glint of VISSER's cigarette lighter underneath the dead fish.

VISSER's hands move over the near part of the desk, picking up the money and the 9 × 12 picture envelope.

EXTREME HIGH SHOT   THE OFFICE

As VISSER turns from the desk and walks across the room out of frame. We hear the back door opening.

VISSER: Who looks stupid now.

The door slams shut.

The only sound is the whir of the fan. A pause. The camera tracks slowly forward, tilting down to keep MARTY *and the desktop centered in frame. As the camera moves the noise of the fan grows louder. When* MARTY's *body and the desk are directly beneath us, the blades of the ceiling fan cut across the immediate foreground and effect a:*

WIPE TO:
MARTY'S BAR   LATER

It is completely still. We are looking from the bar, across the dark empty floor, toward the pebbled windows at the front of the building that catch a hard blue light from the streetlamps outside. The jukebox in the middle distance glows in the darkness.

A pair of headlights catches the pebbled glass and grows brighter as we hear a car pull up to the bar and stop. We hear a car door open and shut, then the sound of feet on gravel. A huge shadow appears on the pebbled glass as the figure crosses in front of the headlights. The man tries the door, finds it locked, and walks back in front of the headlights to cup his hands at a window. He walks back to the door, and a moment later it swings open—framing him in the doorway in silhouette.

We follow him as he moves across the floor, behind the bar and up to the cash register. He switches on a small fluorescent light clamped to the top of the cash register. It is RAY.

He punches a key and the register rings open. He lifts up the empty cash drawer and takes some papers from underneath it.

RAY'S POV

As he flips through the papers: bills, receipts, no money.

BACK TO RAY

As he finishes flipping through the papers.

RAY (*muttering*):   Damn . . .

He slips them back under the cash drawer and slams the register shut. Turning from the register he glances around the bar, then pauses, noticing something.

RAY'S POV

Light is spilling out from under the door to MARTY*'s office.*

BACK TO RAY

As he starts across the floor to MARTY*'s office.*

RAY: Marty . . .

He reaches the door and knocks sharply. No answer. He turns the knob.

. . . Marty.

The door is locked. We hear the muffled whir of the ceiling fan inside.
A pause. RAY *withdraws a ring of keys from his pocket and uses one on the door. The door swings open.*
Over his shoulder we see MARTY, *still at his desk, his back to us. One foot is still propped on the desk.*

RAY: What's the matter, you deaf?

No answer.
RAY *starts toward* MARTY.
He stumbles slightly and we hear the sharp blast of a gun and the sound of something metallic skating across the floor.
RAY, *startled, steadies himself against the desk, then studies* MARTY.

RAY'S POV

There is a dark pool of blood under MARTY*'s chair.*

BACK TO RAY

He looks back up at MARTY, then walks behind his chair and throws a wall switch. The room is bathed in light. His eyes still on MARTY, RAY crosses behind the desk.

RAY'S POV   TRACKING SHOT

The camera moves in a slow arc around the back of MARTY's motionless head.

BACK TO RAY

Still moving. He looks away from MARTY, scans the floor. He gets down on his hands and knees and peers under the safe.

RAY'S POV

There is a glinting silver circle in the darkness under the safe. It is the business end of the revolver that RAY half-stumbled over, half-kicked.

BACK TO RAY

Still on his hands and knees. He reaches in and we hear a rattle as he gropes under the safe. He withdraws the gun, looks at it.

THE GUN

It is ABBY's revolver.

BACK TO RAY

For a long moment he doesn't move. Then, slowly, he starts to get up.

WIDER

The desk, MARTY behind it, RAY straightening behind him. RAY looks from the gun to MARTY, slowly sets the gun down on the desk. A pause. He begins to hoist MARTY from the chair.

There is noise from the bar, as of someone entering.
RAY *reacts.*

THE DOOR

Separating the bar and back office. RAY *hurries to it.*

MEURICE (*os*):   Marty?

Footsteps approach the door.

EXTREME CLOSE SHOT   RAY'S HAND ON THE DOOR BOLT

He turns it gently. The bolt clicks shut.

BACK TO RAY

MEURICE'*s footsteps draw nearer.*

MEURICE (*os*):   Marty, ya home?

There is a rap at the door; RAY *stands frozen. The doorknob rattles.* RAY *reaches out compulsively to grab it, but stops himself before actually touching it.*
    Now MEURICE'*s footsteps can be heard going casually back into the bar. We hold on* RAY'*s rigidly set face.*

MEURICE (*os*):   What day is it today, Angie?

WOMAN (*os*):   Tuesday.

MEURICE (*os*):   Tuesday night is ladies' night.

WOMAN (*os*):   What?

MEURICE (*os*):   Tuesday night is ladies' night. All your drinks are free.

We hear a record drop on the jukebox and a Motown song blares.

RAY crosses to MARTY's chair and takes off his nylon windbreaker. He stoops down and tries to mop up the pool of blood with his windbreaker. This isn't going to work.

He rises and walks over to the bathroom, the windbreaker dripping blood.

MARTY'S OFFICE BATHROOM
CLOSE SHOT   FAUCET

The song continues faintly in the background. The faucet is turned on and RAY's hand enters frame, holding a dirty white towel under the stream of water.

BLOOD-SPATTERED FLOOR

The song continues in the background. RAY's hand enters frame holding the balled-up towel. His windbreaker is wrapped inside. The camera follows as he pushes it across the trail of dripped blood to the pool of blood under MARTY's chair.

CLOSE SHOT   MARTY

He still has not moved. RAY rises into frame and takes him under the armpits. He notices something on the desk in front of him.

CLOSE SHOT   THE GUN ON THE DESK

RAY's hand enters frame and picks it up.

CLOSE SHOT   MARTY'S COAT POCKET

RAY's hand enters frame and slips the gun into MARTY's pocket. MARTY is hoisted up.

EXT   BACK OF THE BAR/PARKING LOT

RAY appears in the doorway. The music from the bar, though fainter, can still be heard.

There are three or four wooden steps going down from the back door to the small gravel parking lot in back. RAY backs down the stairs; MARTY's feet THUMP-THUMP-THUMP down the stairs after him.

The rear door of RAY's car is open. RAY heaves in MARTY's torso. MARTY's legs rest on the ground outside the car. RAY takes an ankle in each hand and pushes.

CLOSE SHOT   RAY

As he shuts the back door. He looks up across the parking lot.

RAY'S POV

The incinerator belching fire and smoke. We hear its distant roar over the bar song. We hear the car door slam.

HIGH-ANGLE TRACKING SHOT   TOWARD INCINERATOR

We are looking down on RAY's car as the camera tracks behind it towards the incinerator. At the cut the roar of the incinerator is suddenly louder. It grows louder still as we approach it.

RAY's car draws even with the incinerator without slowing or stopping. The wadded-up towel is chucked out of his window into the fire. We hold on the fire as RAY's car rolls on out of frame.

INT   RAY'S CAR

As he drives down a deserted country highway. We hear the rhythmic sound of the wheels clomping over asphalt. The radio is broadcasting a fundamentalist's sermon, periodically interrupted by static. RAY is sweating.

EVANGELIST: —so there were three signs, the second of which is Famine, this famine which I have already pointed out is devastatin' Africa and the Indian subcontinent. And the third of these signs is earthquakes. Now I don't know why he threw that in but if you talk to a geologist, and I've talked to many, he'll tell you that earthquake activity—

RAY twists around and looks in the back seat.

RAY'S POV

MARTY is lying inert.

—has increased almost eighty percent in the past two years, and what's more, in two years' time we'll be experiencin' what's known as the Jupiter Effect—

BACK TO RAY

He looks back at the road. A car roars by.

—wherein all the planets of the known universe will be aligned up causin' an incredible buildup of destructive gravitational force. Now in Matthew Chapter Six, Verse Eighteen the Lord out and tells us that these are the signs by which we shall know that He is at our door. There are many good people disagree with me, but it's my belief that this Antichrist is alive today and livin' somewhere in Europe, in that ten-nation alliance I spoke of, bein' groomed for his task—

RAY switches off the radio.
We hear the sound of faint, labored breathing.

EXTREME CLOSE SHOT   RAY

His jaw tightens. He whips his head toward the back seat. His head snaps forward again and he slams on the brakes.
The car screeches to a halt.

EXT   HIGHWAY
LONG SHOT   THE CAR

As RAY's door flies open. He is bolting from the car. The camera, at waist level, tracks toward him as he races out into the field that abuts the highway.

Fifty yards in he finally stops, panting, framed from a low angle. His breath vaporizes in the crisp night air. We hear only his breath and the chirring of crickets. He is looking back toward the road.

RAY'S POV   LONG SHOT   THE CAR

Standing abandoned on the shoulder of the deserted highway. Its headlights cast a lonely beam up the road. No movement.

BACK TO RAY

His panting slows. He is in a cold sweat. After a long moment, he starts walking slowly, reluctantly, back toward the car.

RAY'S POV   TRACKING

Toward the car. Still no sign of movement.

BACK TO RAY

He slows as he draws up to the back of the car. He looks in the back window.

RAY'S POV   BACK SEAT OF THE CAR

It is empty.
   The door on the highway side is ajar.

BACK TO RAY

No reaction.
   He walks around the back of the car onto the highway. He looks up the road.

RAY'S POV

MARTY is crawling up the road on his hands and knees, leaving a trail of blood. The headlights of RAY's car give him a fantastically long shadow.

BACK TO RAY

Still no reaction. He gets into the driver's seat and stares through the windshield as he gropes for the ignition key.

RAY'S POV

MARTY, crawling.

BACK TO RAY

He throws the car into drive, looks at his target, thinks— decides. He pulls the key out of the ignition and goes around to the trunk of the car. He opens it and pulls out a shovel.

MARTY   LOW ANGLE

From in front. The headlights glare behind him. His breath vaporizes. In the background RAY is walking toward him, dragging the shovel, which scrapes along the asphalt. As RAY moves into the foreground and turns to face MARTY only his lower legs and the shovel are in frame.
   The shovel rises out of frame.

CLOSE SHOT   RAY

Both hands hold the shovel tensed over his shoulder. He stares down at MARTY. A long pause. We hear a distant rumble.

CLOSE SHOT   RAY'S FEET

Inches away from MARTY. MARTY's hand slides forward and wraps around one of RAY's ankles.

BACK TO RAY

He shudders. He adjusts his grip on the shovel.
The rumble grows louder.

RAY'S FEET

He jerks his foot away, breaking MARTY'*s grasp.*

BACK TO RAY

Looks up from MARTY*. The rumble grows louder.*

RAY'S POV

Headlight beams, although not yet the headlights themselves,
are visible a long way down the road.

BACK TO RAY

Staring down the road. Finally he lowers the shovel, walks
back to the car and throws it viciously into the trunk, walks
back up into the foreground and stoops down.

CLOSE SHOT   MARTY

As RAY *grabs him under the armpits and starts dragging him*
back to the car. Just before RAY *heaves him into the back seat,*
MARTY *coughs weakly. A fine spray of blood comes out with*
the cough.
The engine rumble is quite loud now.

MED SHOT   RAY   FROM ACROSS THE ROOF OF THE CAR

As he slams the back door shut. He presses himself against
the side of his car. Headlights glare over him; the truck roars
by just behind him.

EXT   OPEN FIELD
FULL SHOT   RAY'S CAR

Sudden quiet at the cut. We are looking at RAY'*s car in*
profile, parked in the middle of a deserted field. From

offscreen we hear the sound of a shovel biting into earth.

We track laterally down the car, along the beam of its headlights, to finally frame RAY as he climbs out of the shallow grave he has just finished digging.

He plants the shovel and walks back to the car.

VERY WIDE SHOT

The grave in the middle background; the car's headlights beyond it.

RAY is dragging MARTY toward the grave. He dumps him in.

HIGH SHOT   THE GRAVE

As MARTY thumps to the bottom, face up.

CLOSE SHOT   RAY

As he bends over to pick up the shovel, dripping sweat. We hear the shovel biting into earth.

HIGH SHOT   THE GRAVE

RAY, in the foreground, pitches the first shovelful of earth onto MARTY. MARTY moves slightly.

LOW SHOT   RAY

As he pauses, looking down into the grave. He stoops down and resumes shoveling, bobbing in and out of frame as he hurls dirt into the grave.

BACK TO HIGH SHOT

As RAY shovels, MARTY is moving under the loose dirt. A faint, inarticulate noise comes from the grave.

Almost imperceptibly, MARTY's right arm starts to rise.

LOW SHOT   FROM INSIDE THE GRAVE

RAY stands on the lip of the grave, hunched over his shovel, crisply illuminated by the headlights. In the shadowy *foreground* MARTY's *arm rises, extended toward* RAY. *He is clutching* ABBY's *gun in his splint-fingered hand.*

CLOSE SHOT   RAY

As he straightens up and stands motionless, expressionless, watching MARTY, *making no attempt to get out of the way.*

HIGH SHOT   MARTY

The gun extended into the foreground. His index finger splinted, he slides his middle finger over the trigger of the gun.

LOW SHOT   RAY

Watching.

HIGH SHOT   MARTY

The gun trembling in the foreground. His knuckle whitens over the trigger.
    The trigger releases and we hear the dull click of an empty chamber.

LOW SHOT   RAY

Staring blankly down at MARTY.

SIDE SHOT

Of MARTY's *gun hand as* RAY *slowly sinks down on the lip of the grave, bracing himself with the shovel. His hand reaches for* MARTY's. MARTY *squeezes off two more empty chambers.* RAY's *hand slowly closes over the barrel of the gun.*
    As he pulls, the gun slides from MARTY's *fingers.*

CLOSE SHOT   THE BLADE OF THE SHOVEL

Biting into the earth.

MED SHOT   RAY

Furiously shoveling dirt into the grave.

HIGH SHOT   THE GRAVE

MARTY barely visible under the dirt.

MED SHOT   RAY

Shoveling, panting.

HIGH SHOT   THE GRAVE

Half full.

MED SHOT   RAY

Working furiously. His breath comes in short gasps.

HIGH SHOT   THE GRAVE

It is filled. RAY is packing down the earth, slamming the shovel furiously against the bare patch of earth.

CLOSE SHOT   THE BLADE OF THE SHOVEL

Being slammed down against the earth. Again and again.

EXT   OPEN FIELD   SUNRISE

The staccato beat of the shovel slamming against earth drops out at the cut. There is perfect quiet. The sun is just peeping over the horizon. In the foreground RAY is sitting in the open door of his car, smoking a cigarette. His gaze is fixed on a spot offscreen.

HIS POV

A house. Quite near by.
    The house and its perfect green rectangle of lawn are set incongruously in the middle of the open field.

BACK TO RAY

Staring, without emotion.

He takes one last, fierce drag on the cigarette, then flicks it away. He takes the shovel, walks over to the grave and stares at it for several seconds, shovel clasped firmly in both hands.

He walks back to the car.

HIGH SHOT

House, car and grave. RAY *throws the shovel into the car, gets in, and turns the ignition.*

The engine coughs weakly and dies.

He tries again. Same result.

One more time. The engine coughs, sputters, and fires to life. The car runs over the grave and rattles on across the rutted field towards the highway in the distance.

INT RAY'S CAR DAWN

As RAY *drives down the straight empty highway in the flat early-morning light.*

CLOSE SHOT RAY

Pale and unblinking.

RAY'S POV THE HIGHWAY

In the distance we see a beat-up white station wagon approaching. Its headlights wink on, then off again.

BACK TO RAY

He squints at the approaching car.

RAY'S POV

The car is closer. Its headlights wink again.

BACK TO RAY

His jaw tightens. He stares intently at the car. Then, abruptly, he looks down at his dashboard.

CLOSE SHOT   HEADLIGHT KNOB ON THE DASHBOARD

His headlights are on. RAY's *hand enters frame and pushes in the knob.*

SIDE ANGLE   RAY

Watching the approaching station wagon. As it passes we catch a glimpse of its occupant. He grins and cocks a you-got-it finger at RAY *before roaring on out of frame.*

EXT   DESERTED GAS STATION
HIGH ANGLE

The station hasn't opened yet. RAY's *car, empty, stands alone in the lot. Flat prairie stretches to the horizon. No movement in the frame.*

   At the cut we hear the faint sound of a phone ringing through a receiver. After four or five rings the phone is picked up and we begin a slow crane down.

ABBY (*through phone; sleepily*):   Hello?

RAY (*present; very hoarsely*):   Abby . . . you all right?

ABBY: Ray? . . . What time is it?

RAY: I don't know. It's early . . . I love you.

   A beat.

ABBY: . . . You all right?

RAY: I don't know. I better get off now.

   The continuing crane down reveals RAY *in a phone booth in the foreground.*

ABBY: Okay, see ya . . . Thanks, Ray.

RAY: Abby—

The phone disconnects.

INT   ABBY'S APARTMENT
CLOSE SHOT   ABBY

Her sleeping head on a pillow. Offscreen we hear a door open and shut. A moment later RAY's dirt-caked hand comes into frame and gently brushes a wisp of hair back from ABBY's face. We hear RAY walk across the apartment and a moment later the sound of water running.
   ABBY stirs. She looks offscreen.

LONG SHOT   RAY

Standing in the doorway to the bathroom. He is wiping his hands on a towel.

ABBY (*sleepily*):   . . . Ray?

RAY: You're bad.

Still half asleep, ABBY smiles.

ABBY: . . . What?

RAY: I said you're bad.

There is a long pause. Finally:

ABBY (*smiling*):   . . . You're bad too.

RAY swings a chair out and sits down behind a table at the far end of the room. He leans back and props his legs up on the table. He is staring across the room at ABBY.

RAY: We're both bad.

FADE OUT

BLACK

As we hear the click of a pull-string the camera is dropping: down past an orange safe light, down the length of its string, down to a metal darkroom tray where two short strips of negative are burning.

VISSER's hand and yellow sleeve cuff (now orange) enter frame, with an 8 × 10 black-and-white photograph. The photograph is dropped into the tray. As it burns we see that it is the same picture of ABBY's and RAY's "corpses" as VISSER showed MARTY, except that in this print the bullet holes and blood are less convincingly brushed in.

Another print is dropped into the tray and ignites. In this one we see bullet holes but no blood.

A third print is dropped in and ignites. It is the original undoctored shot of ABBY and RAY asleep in bed.

VISSER's hands enter frame holding the picture-envelope that he took away from MARTY's office. VISSER rips it in half and is about to drop it into the tray, but stops abruptly.

There is posterboard, not a photograph, peeking out of the torn envelope.

VISSER's hands pull the two halves of the placard from the envelope and fit them together. The stenciled 8 × 10 placard says: "All Employees Must Wash Hands Before Resuming Work."

LOW-ANGLE CLOSE SHOT   VISSER

Staring at the placard in disbelief.

After a moment his hand rises into frame to deposit a cigarette in his mouth. His hand drops back down, groping in a pocket.

His hand jumps back into frame, empty; he thumps at his breast pockets; he can't find his lighter.

He wheels and exits frame. The light snaps off. A door slams shut.

ABBY'S APARTMENT   DAY
CLOSE SHOT   RAY

He has dozed off in his chair. Offscreen we hear a door slam, and his eyes open.

ABBY

Emerging from the bathroom. Her voice has a flat echo in the bare apartment.

ABBY: Why didn't you get into bed?

RAY (*groggy*):   I didn't think I could sleep. I'm surprised you could. Are you all right?

ABBY: Yeah . . .

She walks over and sits down on the bed.

. . . You called me this morning.

RAY: Yeah.

ABBY looks at him, expecting more. Finally:

. . . I just wanted to let you know that everything was all right. I took care of everything. Now all we have to do is keep our heads.

ABBY: . . . What do you mean?

RAY finally looks directly at her.

RAY: I know about it, Abby. I went to the bar last night.

ABBY is looking at him in alarm.

ABBY: What happened?—Was Meurice there?

RAY: Yeah.

He laughs shortly.

. . . He didn't see me, though. Nobody saw me.

The chair grates back as he stands up and looks vaguely around the room.

. . . Is it cold in here?

ABBY *is looking at him nervously.*

ABBY: Well . . . what happened?

RAY: I cleaned it all up, but that ain't important . . .

He starts nervously pacing around the room, looking for something.

. . . What's important is what we do now; I mean we can't go around half-cocked. What we need is some time to think about this, figure it out . . .

He moves a packing crate aside, still hunting around the apartment.

. . . Anyway, we got some time now. But we gotta be smart.

ABBY: Ray—

RAY: Abby, never point a gun at anyone unless you're gonna shoot him. And when you shoot him you better make sure he's dead . . .

RAY's pacing is more agitated as he looks distractedly around the apartment.

RAY:　　. . . because if he's not dead he's gonna get up and try and kill you.

He pauses, seemingly at a total loss.

　. . . That's the only thing they told us in the service that was worth a goddamn—Where the hell's my windbreaker?

ABBY:　　What the hell happened, Ray?

RAY is walking to the window. Sunlight streams in around him.

RAY:　　That ain't important. What's important is that we did it. That's the only thing that matters. We both did it for each other . . .

He stoops down to look through a pile of clothes by the window.

　. . . That's what's important.

ABBY:　　I don't know what you're talking about.

RAY's head snaps around. Staring at her he slowly rises to his feet and then remains still.

ABBY:　　I . . . I mean what're you talking about, Ray? *I* haven't done anything funny.

RAY:　　. . . *What* was that?

ABBY, startled, can't contain her agitation anymore.

ABBY (*rapidly*):   Ray, I mean you ain't even acting like yourself. First you call me at five in the A.M. saying all kinds of nice things over the telephone and then you come charging in here scaring me half to death without even telling me what it is I'm supposed to be scared of. I gotta tell you it's extremely rattling.

RAY

We track toward him, isolating him against the window. He is perfectly still. For a long time he can't speak.

RAY (*quietly*):   . . . Don't lie to me, Abby—

BACK TO ABBY

Still worked up.

ABBY: How can I be lying if I don't even know—

The ring of the telephone cuts her off. She looks at the phone, pauses for a moment, then continues, struggling.

John Getz

. . . I mean if you and him had a fight or something, I don't care, as long as you . . .

Her voice trails off.
The telephone won't stop ringing. ABBY *and* RAY *are staring at each other, seemingly oblivious to it. Finally:*

RAY: . . . Pick it up.

CLOSE SHOT   THE TELEPHONE

Still ringing. ABBY's *hand enters frame and picks it up.*

ABBY: What.

Through the phone we hear only the rhythmic whir of a ceiling fan. ABBY *shifts the phone to her other ear, listening hard. It is the same sound we heard earlier when she picked up the phone at* RAY's *house.*
As before, the line clicks dead.

ABBY (*looking at* RAY):   . . . Welp, that was him.

There is a long moment of silence. Then RAY's *voice comes from across the room:*

RAY: . . . Who?

ABBY: Marty.

There is silence again.

LONG SHOT   THE APARTMENT

RAY *shifts in front of the window. He laughs humorlessly. The laugh stops abruptly.*

ABBY: . . . What's going on with you two?

RAY (*quietly*):   All right . . .

He starts across the room.

. . . You can call him back, whoever it was . . .

He is heading for the door.

. . . I'll get out of your way.

He pauses at the foyer and pulls ABBY's gun out of his pocket. He sets it on a shelf by the door.

ABBY

Watching. We hear the door open.

RAY (*os*):   You left your weapon behind.

We hear the door slam shut.

CLOSE SHOT   CEILING FAN

We hear the rhythmic whir of the fan. We tilt down from the ceiling to reveal that we are in the living room of RAY's bungalow.

   In the foreground VISSER sits in a chair with the cradled telephone in his lap, facing the front door, which stands open in the background. The contents of ABBY's tote bag lie strewn on the bureau next to VISSER. Her purse is not there. After a moment VISSER rouses himself and starts to sweep the articles back into the tote bag.

INT   MEURICE'S APARTMENT   DAY
LOW WIDE SHOT   LIVING ROOM

It is dark, lit only by the morning light leaking in around the drawn blinds. It is a small modern apartment such as one sees in large apartment complexes—shag carpeting, built-in

*bar. In the extreme foreground the small red "Power" light of
a telephone answering machine glows in the darkness.*

*The front door opens in the background, spilling bright
sunlight.* MEURICE *stoops down, picks up two newspapers,
enters, and shuts the door. He walks toward the camera and
his hand enters frame in extreme foreground to punch the
rewind button on the machine. His hand leaves frame. A few
pieces of mail are flipped down onto the machine table, piece
by piece, as the machine rewinds. He reaches down again and
hits playback. After a beep:*

WOMAN'S VOICE: Hi Meurice, this is Helene, Helene
Trend, and I'm calling 'cause I wanna know just what the
hell that remark you made about Sylvia's supposed to
mean . . .

Mail continues to flip down onto the table, piece by piece.

. . . She says you're full of shit and frankly I believe
her. And hey, I love you too. Sure. Anyway, you better
call me soon because I'm going to South America
tonight—you know, Uruguay?

Dial tone. Beep.

MARTY'S VOICE (*barking*):   Listen asshole, you know
who this is. I just got back from Corpus and there's a lot
of money missing from the safe . . .

The mail stops dropping; MARTY *has* MEURICE'S *attention.*

. . . I'm not saying you took it but the place was your
responsibility and I told you to keep an eye on your
asshole friend. Don't—uh, don't come to the bar tonight,
I've got a meeting. But tomorrow I want to have a word
with you, and with Ray—if you can find him.

Dial tone. Beep.
   MEURICE's *hand drops into frame.*

WOMAN'S VOICE: Meurice, where the hell have you
been? I—

His finger presses the stop button.

MATCH CUT TO:
RAY'S FINGER

*Pressing into a dark stain in the upholstery of the back seat of
his car. When he raises it the fingertip is red—the seat still
wet with blood.*

CLOSE SHOT   RAY

*Looking down at the seat. He backs out of the car and walks
up the driveway to his house.*

INT   RAY'S LIVING ROOM

*As he comes through the screen door. It bangs shut behind
him. As he crosses the living room we see, and he hears,*
MEURICE's *Trans Am pulling up and stopping at the foot of
the lawn.* RAY *turns and looks out the window.*

CLOSE SHOT   CLOSET DOOR

RAY *throws it open and hurriedly pulls out the first thing at
hand—a sheet. We hear the door of the Trans Am open and
slam shut.*

EXT   RAY'S BUNGALOW
TRACKING SHOT   ON RAY

*Exiting the house as the screen door bangs and shudders
behind him. He hurries down the walk.*

TRACKING SHOT   RAY'S POV

MEURICE *is rounding the bottom of the lawn and starting up the drive toward the incriminating car. Its back door is standing ajar.*

MEURICE: I hope you're planning on leaving town.

BACK TO RAY

Reacting to the line as he reaches the car. He bends over to throw the sheet over the seat just as MEURICE *walks up behind him.*

RAY (*his back to* MEURICE; *arranging the sheet*):   Got a problem, Meurice?

MEURICE: No, you do, cowboy. You been to the bar?

RAY *is still hunched in the open doorway. He freezes momentarily in arranging the sheet.*

RAY: . . . Why?

MEURICE: You shouldn't have taken the money . . .

RAY *doesn't reply or turn around.* MEURICE *is getting more strident.*

. . . Look at me man, I'm serious. You broke in the bar and ripped off the safe . . .

RAY *backs out of the car and turns around.*

. . . Abby warned me you were gonna make trouble. Trouble with you is, you're too fucking obvious; the only ones with the combination are me and you . . .

RAY *looks evenly at* MEURICE. *Behind him the sheet has been arranged over the seat. He puts an unlit cigarette in his mouth.*

. . . and Abby. Maybe. But as far as I'm concerned that only leaves one fucking possibility.

RAY (*tonelessly*):   What's that?

MEURICE *reaches out and swipes the unlit cigarette out of* RAY's *mouth.*

MEURICE: Those things are nothing but coffin nails.

He turns and stares down the street, exasperated.

Samm-Art Williams and John Getz

. . . Look. Personally I don't give a shit. I know
Marty's a hard-on but you gotta do something. I don't
know; give the money back, say you're sorry, or get the
fuck out of here, or something . . .

*Now that his temper is gone, he realizes he has nothing much
to say. He shakes his head and turns back down the drive,
muttering as he lights himself* RAY's *cigarette.*

. . . It's very humiliating, preaching about this shit.

CLOSE SHOT RAY

Standing in front of the back door of his car, watching
MEURICE *walk away. His right hand rises into frame to
deposit another unlit cigarette in his mouth. Offscreen,*
MEURICE *calls from the end of the drive:*

MEURICE: I'm not laughing at this, Ray Bob, so you
know it's no fucking joke.

We hear his car door slam. After a moment RAY *exits frame,
heading for the house. The camera tracks slowly in to the back
window of the car.*
   *Traces of blood are starting to seep up from the upholstery
into the sheet.*

INT MARTY'S HOUSE DAY
LOW WIDE SHOT FRONT FOYER

*We are looking across the tiled floor toward the front
doorway. The room has the dim gray cast of daytime inside a
shuttered house. We hold on the empty foyer as we hear an
intermittent high whining sound. We hear the padding of feet
on carpet, and then the clatter of nails on tile as Opal,*
MARTY's *German shepherd, trots into frame and circles the
foyer, still whining. She jumps up and scratches desperately
at the front door.*
   A slow, rhythmic pounding is very faint on the track.

EXT   MARTY'S BAR   DUSK

ABBY has just gotten out of her car and is walking up to the front of the darkened bar. The faint, rhythmic thumping continues over the cut, its source somewhere offscreen. As ABBY takes a key out of her purse and lets herself into the bar, the thumping stops.

INT   MARTY'S BAR

ABBY switches on the lights, looks around, goes to the back-office door. Locked. As she fits her key into the lock:

ABBY (*quietly*):   Marty?

The door swings open, fanning a shaft of light into the darkened room.

MARTY'S OFFICE BATHROOM

We are looking from the inside at the bathroom door that won't close all the way. As the light fans into the office beyond and seeps in through the crack of the bathroom door, we see VISSER's sleeve cuff and his hand pressing against the door, to hold it near-shut.

BACK TO ABBY

Standing in the office doorway. We pull her into the room. She stops abruptly, looking past the camera, and wrinkles her nose.

ABBY'S POV

MARTY's fish, now half-decayed, still lie on the desk.
  Some of the desk drawers stand open, with some of their contents strewn across the surface of the desk.

BACK TO ABBY

She takes a step forward. We hear the crunch of glass underfoot. She looks down at the floor.

ABBY'S POV

Shards of broken glass lie on the floor.

BACK TO ABBY

She looks up from the floor toward the back door.

ABBY'S POV

The pane of the back-door window closest to the knob has been shattered from the outside, scattering broken glass into the office.

BACK TO ABBY

She crosses slowly to the desk, staring at the rotted fish. She looks up from the desk.

ABBY'S POV

On the standing safe behind the desk lies a white towel. ABBY's hand enters frame and picks up the towel.
    In slow motion a hammer that's been wrapped inside slips out of the towel, falls end-over-end, hits the floor with a dull thud.

BACK TO ABBY

Stooping down to pick up the hammer. At eye level as she stoops down is the combination dial to the safe. The dial has been battered by the hammer. ABBY looks from the hammer to the floor under the desk chair.

ABBY'S POV

Blood stains.

ABBY

Staring down at the floor. She rises and looks at the desk. As she rises we hear glass under her feet.

ABBY'S POV

The dead fish. Beyond them, on the floor around the desk, broken glass.

BACK TO ABBY

Staring.

ABBY'S POV

The dead fish.

BACK TO ABBY

She seems to be falling slowly backwards. The camera falls with her, keeping her in close shot. Her head hits a pillow. We pull back slowly to reveal that she is lying on the bed in her apartment, staring across the room. She lies motionless on the bed, her eyes wide.

ABBY'S POV

Across the darkened apartment we see the curtainless windows, and beyond them, across the lamplit street, the facade of the opposite building.

LONG SHOT   ABBY

Lying still. After a moment she gets out of bed, crosses to the front door of the apartment, locks it, then walks unsteadily back to the bed.

FADE OUT

FADE IN:
SAME LONG SHOT   ABBY IN BED

She opens her eyes, lies still for a moment, coughs. She gets out of bed and walks across the still dark apartment to the bathroom. She shuts the bathroom door.

BATHROOM

ABBY *looks at herself in the mirror above the sink, then turns
on the tap water. From a neighboring apartment we hear a
dull rhythmic thumping on the wall. She pauses, listens for a
moment, then starts to splash water on her face.*

*From somewhere offscreen we hear the sharp sound of glass
shattering. It reverberates for a moment, then dies.* ABBY
*looks up at the bathroom door. We hear a scraping at the lock
of her apartment door.* ABBY *listens.*

*Suddenly we hear the lock springing open, and the front
door swinging on its hinges.*

CLOSE SHOT ABBY

*Startled. She shuts off the water and stands motionless.
Droplets of water are streaming down her face.*

*We hear the sound of footsteps in the next room, crunching
across broken glass.*

ABBY: Ray. . . ?

*There is no answer. After a moment we hear bedsprings creak
in the next room.* ABBY *opens the bathroom door and walks
out.*

MAIN ROOM

*A shaft of light slices across the floor from the open bathroom
door. Broken glass glints on the floor. In the semi-darkness
we can see that someone is sitting on the bed. The person
looks up.*

It is MARTY.
ABBY *recoils.*

MARTY: Lover-boy oughta lock his door.

ABBY *looks nervously at* MARTY. *Droplets of water are still
running down her face. She brushes one from her eye.*

MARTY: I love you . . .

He smiles thinly.

. . . That's a stupid thing to say, right?

ABBY takes a step back.

ABBY: I . . . I love you too.

Still smiling, MARTY shakes his head.

MARTY: No. You're just saying that because you're
scared . . .

*He stands. We hear glass under his feet. He unbuttons the
middle button of his coat and reaches inside.*

. . . You left your weapon behind.

*He withdraws something from an inside pocket and tosses it
to her.*

CLOSE SHOT   ABBY'S HANDS

As she catches the object. It is her compact.

CLOSE SHOT   ABBY

She looks from her hands up to MARTY.

MARTY: He'll kill you too.

*MARTY gags, leans forward, doubles over to vomit—blood.
The blood washes over the floor at his feet.*

ABBY

*Bolts upright in bed with a muffled groan. Sweat pours down
her face. She brushes a drop of sweat from her eye and looks
around.*

ABBY'S POV

Moonlight glints through the windows across the hardwood floor. Through the windows we can see the facade of the opposite building. The apartment is dark and still, just as we left it before she fell asleep.

BACK TO ABBY

She slumps back onto the bed. One hand gropes down out of frame and comes up holding an illuminated alarm clock. She looks at it, drops it back to the floor.

She turns on her side and stares across the room toward the window.

ABBY'S POV

The window.

DISSOLVE THROUGH TO:
SAME WINDOW   SAME ANGLE   PRE-DAWN

It is still not quite light. The few lights that shined in the windows of the opposite building before are now off; the facade of the building is a flat, undetailed gray.

CLOSE SHOT   ABBY

Still lying on her side on the bed, her eyes open, staring at the window.

BACK TO LONG SHOT   WINDOW

After a moment ABBY *enters frame. She picks her coat off a chair and puts it on.*

We hear a car door slam.

EXT   RAY'S BUNGALOW   PRE-DAWN

ABBY *has just gotten out of her car in the foreground and is crossing the lawn to the house. Down the road the street lights are still on. One light burns in the house, in the window of* RAY's *bedroom.* ABBY *approaches it.*

THROUGH THE WINDOW

Over ABBY's *shoulder, as she leans against the sill of the open window and looks inside.*

RAY *sits on the bed in the empty room, smoking a cigarette, his profile to the window, gazing fixedly at the wall.*

ABBY: Ray.

RAY *starts and looks toward the window, squinting.*

INT   RAY'S BUNGALOW
WIDE SHOT   LIVING ROOM

ABBY *is coming through the screen door. The room is strikingly bare of everything except furniture. All personal effects have been removed.*

ABBY *looks around, bewildered, as* RAY *enters from the hallway.*

ABBY: . . . Where is everything?

RAY: In the trunk.

ABBY, *still standing in front of the door, looks at him uncomprehendingly.* RAY *walks over to a couple of cardboard boxes stacked in the corner.*

. . . In the car.

He ties a knot around the top carton with a piece of cord, then cuts the cord with a collapsible fishing knife.

ABBY: . . . You leaving?

RAY: Isn't that what you want?

She slowly shakes her head.

RAY: Wanna come with me?

He leans back against the boxes, watching her.

ABBY: . . . But first I gotta know what happened.

RAY: What do you want to know?

ABBY: You broke into the bar. You wanted to get your money. You and Marty had a fight. Something happened . . .

RAY shakes his head, smiling. ABBY squints at him, looking for help.

. . . I don't know, *wasn't* it you? Maybe a burglar broke in, and you found—

RAY: With your gun? . . .

He puts the knife in his pocket and walks over to the door. As he approaches her:

. . . Nobody broke in, Abby. I'll tell you the truth . . .

RAY faces ABBY in front of the door.

RAY: . . . Truth is, I've felt sick the last couple of days. Can't eat . . . Can't sleep . . . When I try to I . . . Abby . . .

It's difficult to bring it out. RAY's hand gropes for the cross-slat on the screen door. Finally:

. . . The truth is . . . he was alive when I buried him.

ABBY *stares.*

An object materializes in the sky beyond them. It is flipping end-over-end in slow motion, moving toward ABBY *and* RAY *and the screen door.* ABBY *and* RAY, *each staring at the other, fail to notice it until—*

THWACK—it bounces off the screen.

ABBY *starts;* RAY *doesn't.*

The spell broken, ABBY *pushes hesitantly at the screen door.* RAY's *hand slides off the cross-slat; he makes no move to stop her.*

CLOSE SHOT   THE FRONT STOOP

As ABBY *steps over the rolled-up newspaper that hit the screen door.*

TRACKING SHOT   ON ABBY

Hurrying down the driveway to get to her car. A low rumble is building on the soundtrack. ABBY *glances at* RAY's *car as she passes it.*

ABBY'S POV   TRACKING FORWARD   THE CAR

More blood has seeped into and dried on the dropsheet covering the back seat. The bass rumble grows louder, punctuated by a rhythmic thumping.

EXT   MEURICE'S APARTMENT   DAY
OVER ABBY'S SHOULDER

As she pounds frantically on the door—the sound continuing over the cut. After a moment the door edges open.

MEURICE *is standing in the doorway in a long bathrobe. A sleeper's blindfold is pushed up over his forehead.*

MEURICE: Abby. What's the matter?

ABBY: I . . . I'm sorry, Meurice. I gotta talk to you . . . Can I come in?

He looks at her hard.

MEURICE: Yeah . . . yeah, come in . . .

He steps aside to let her pass.

. . . but I gotta tell ya . . .

INT   MEURICE'S APARTMENT

As ABBY enters.

MEURICE: . . . I'm retired.

MEURICE *switches on a table lamp; the curtains are drawn against the sun.* ABBY *follows* MEURICE *over to the bar.*

MEURICE: Jesus, I got a hangover. Want a drink?

ABBY: No, I—

MEURICE: Well I do . . .

He pours himself a drink.

. . . For you I answer the door. If you wanna stay here, that's fine. But I'm retired.

ABBY: Something happened with Marty and Ray—

MEURICE (*sharply*):   Abby . . .

He glares at her.

. . . Let me ask you one question . . .

He slams back his drink.

. . . Why do you think I'm retired?

He grimaces.

. . . Ray stole a shitload of money from the Marty.
Until both of 'em calm down I'm not getting involved.

ABBY: No Meurice, it's worse than that. Something
really happened, I think Marty's dead—

MEURICE: What?! Did Ray tell you that?

ABBY: Sort of . . .

MEURICE sits her down on the sofa.

MEURICE: That's total bullshit. Marty called me *after* he
was jacked up . . .

He tries to coax her into lying down.

. . . I mean, I don't know where he is, but he ain't
dead.

ABBY: Meurice—

MEURICE: You don't look too good. You sleep last
night?

Her head meets an end cushion.

ABBY: Meurice, you gotta help me . . .

MEURICE rises from the sofa, sighs.

MEURICE: All right. Just sit tight. Try to get some
sleep . . .

He leans down to the table next to the sofa.

. . . I'll find Marty, find out what's going on.

CLOSE SHOT   ABBY

Her head on the cushion. We hear engine rumble. ABBY *twists her head back, following* MEURICE. *As we hear the table lamp being switched off we:*

CUT TO:
EXT   HIGHWAY   NIGHT
POV FROM A CAR

The engine rumble continues over the cut. There is no other traffic on the highway. A light fog covers the road. A green highway sign says: "San Antonio 73 mi." We hear a car radio playing softly.

CLOSE SHOT   RAY

Driving. He is gently lit by the light from the dashboard. He reaches forward to turn off the radio. The only sound now is the hum of the engine and the rhythmic clomping of tires on pavement. The look and sound of the scene are close to those of the first scene of the movie.

*   RAY *takes a cigarette out of his pocket and puts it in his mouth, but leaves it unlit.*

RAY'S POV

The headlights of an approaching car materialize in the fog. The car passes with a roar.

*   *Up ahead a traffic light is just turning amber.*

BACK TO RAY

The engine hum drops as he slows. We hear the low engine rumble and the squeaking brakes of another car. RAY *is now stopped in front of the deserted intersection. He looks up in his rearview mirror.*

RAY'S POV

Another car is stopped just behind him, the fog floating up past its headlights. The headlights halate in the fog; none of the rest of the car is visible.

BACK TO RAY

The unlit cigarette still in his mouth. He looks down from the rearview mirror to the intersection ahead of him. There is a long pause, during which we hear only the steady purr of RAY's car and the knocking rumble of the car behind him.

   RAY looks up at the traffic light.

RAY'S POV

The light is just turning from red to green.

CLOSE SHOT   RAY'S FOOT ON BRAKE

He takes his foot off the brake, hesitates for a moment, then replaces it on the brake.

CLOSE SHOT   RAY

He looks up in his rearview mirror.

RAY'S POV

The headlights of the other car remain motionless behind him. The car makes no move to pass.

BACK TO RAY

He slowly takes the cigarette from his mouth and drops it onto the seat next to him. His eyes shift from the rearview mirror to the traffic light.

RAY'S POV

Green fog floats up past the green light.

BACK TO RAY

His face frozen. He turns slowly to look behind.

RAY'S POV

The other car is still motionless. We hear the muted rumble of its engine.

BACK TO RAY

His eyes shift back to the mirror. He gropes for his window handle and slowly rolls it down. He sticks out his left arm, eyes still on the rearview mirror, and waves for the other car to go around him.

RAY'S POV

The other car remains still for a moment. White fog floats up beyond the red fog created by RAY's brake lights.
Finally the car pulls out slowly to the left to pass.

BACK TO RAY

Watching the car pass.

RAY'S POV

As the car pulls out into the light from the intersection and RAY's headlights, we see that it is a battered green Volkswagen. First the car itself, and then its red tail lights, disappear into the fog.

BACK TO RAY

Watching, for a long moment.
Finally he takes his foot off the brake, turns the steering wheel hard left and hangs a U-turn.

MARTY'S LIVING ROOM   WIDE

A light is switched on in the expensively appointed room. MEURICE enters, walking silently on the carpet, looking

*around the room. He throws the light off at the far end and
leaves.*

MARTY'S BEDROOM   WIDE

The door swings open. MEURICE *throws the switch near the
door and the room is bathed in light. We are once again in the
bedroom where we earlier saw* ABBY *looking through her
purses.*

We start to hear the faint buzzing of a fly.

MEURICE *glances around, throws off the light, and shuts
the door. Black.*

MARTY'S OFFICE

*Somewhere offscreen a light is switched on and we are looking
in close shot at the dead fish.*

The sound of the fly is louder with the cut.

CLOSE SHOT   RAY

*Standing in the doorway from the bar, staring down at the
fish.*

WIDE SHOT   THE OFFICE

RAY *glances around at the broken glass lying on the floor. His
gaze shifts to the safe and the hammer in front of it. He walks
over to the safe and stoops down.*

CLOSE SHOT   RAY AT SAFE

*He works its battered dial and it swings open. He shuffles
through the contents and brings out a small pile of
photographs.*

RAY'S POV

As he flips through the photographs. The first four are RAY
and ABBY *in the motel room bed. The last is a mounted 8 ×
10:* ABBY *and* MARTY *on a Gulf beach.*

BACK TO RAY

Looking.

HIS POV   PICTURE DETAIL

MARTY is still laughing.

BACK TO RAY

He scowls at the shots VISSER took, then puts them back in the safe. When his hand comes out he is holding another photograph—this one folded twice. He unfolds it.

RAY'S POV

His and ABBY's corpses.

BACK TO RAY   FROM ACROSS THE DESK

As he straightens slowly from the safe in the background.
    At desk level, we again see the glint of VISSER's lighter under the dead fish.
    RAY crosses slowly around the desk into the foreground and lays the picture flat on the desktop. For a moment he stares down at it, then wheels abruptly and leaves frame.

INT   RAY'S CAR
CLOSE SHOT   RAY

Driving. He glances up in the rearview mirror.

MARTY'S KITCHEN

As MEURICE enters and throws an overhead light. The white room is bathed in bright, shadowless light. As MEURICE steps into the kitchen his foot strikes something on the floor below frame, which clatters hollowly away.

CLOSE SHOT   PLASTIC DOG-FOOD BOWL

The empty bowl skids into a wall, bounces back, and wobbles, spinning on its bottom rim.

MARTY'S BILLIARD ROOM
DUTCH-TILT
TRACKING SHOT   TOWARD MOUNTED MOOSE HEAD

On a low skewed axis the camera is tracking in toward the impassive trophy head on MARTY's *billiard-room wall.*

The moose still has RAY's *cigarette protruding from its mouth.*

REVERSE TRACKING SHOT   MEURICE

As he walks toward the moose, head cocked to one side, frowning quizzically up.

He hears something, and looks through the door to his left.

MEURICE'S POV

The long shadowy hall. We hear panting.

CLOSE SHOT   MEURICE

Squinting.

MEURICE: . . . Opal?

THE HALLWAY

A form starts to materialize in the shadows.

MEURICE

Taking a step back.

HIS POV

The dog bounding down the hallway. Its panting has become a low growl.

FROM BEHIND MEURICE

He wrenches a cue stick from the rack and squares.

HIS POV

Opal snarling, leaping.

INT   MEURICE'S APARTMENT
CLOSE SHOT   TOP OF A COFFEE TABLE

The splintered top half of the pool cue is slammed down to rest on top of the coffee table.

MEURICE (*os*):   Even the fucking dog's gone crazy . . .

MED SHOT   ABBY

Sitting on the sofa, looking down out of frame. Behind her MEURICE agitatedly paces back and forth, waving the splintered bottom half of the cue stick. His voice is unnaturally loud.

MEURICE: . . . Something pretty fucking weird is going on. Put your coat on and I'll drop you at home. But don't talk to either of 'em until I do. And don't worry. Believe me. These things always have a logical explanation. Usually.

ABBY'S POV

The splintered top half of the cue stick on the coffee table.

INT   ABBY'S HALLWAY

ABBY approaches her door in the foreground and lets herself in.

INT   ABBY'S APARTMENT

Looking toward the window. The room is dark. Through the window we see the facade of the building across the street. ABBY enters frame in the foreground, in silhouette against the window, and throws an overhead light switch. The bright light reveals RAY standing by the window, looking out.

RAY (*abruptly*):   Turn it off.

ABBY jumps, startled.

ABBY: Ray . . .

EXT   ROOF OF FACING APARTMENT BUILDING

*From the roof of the building across the street we are looking
down on the facade of* ABBY'*s building. Most of its windows
are dark, but in a brightly lit fourth-floor window we can
clearly see* ABBY *and* RAY.

*A man is on the roof in the foreground, hitching a rifle to
his shoulder.*

INT   ABBY'S APARTMENT

RAY *turns from the window which, with the switching on of
the overhead light, has become a mirror of the interior of the
apartment.*

RAY: Just turn it off.

EXT   FACING ROOF

*The light goes out in the apartment across the street; its
window goes opaque.*

INT   ABBY'S APARTMENT

Dark now. RAY *still stands by the window, looking out.* ABBY
still stands by the light switch.

RAY (*answering a question*):   No curtains on the windows.

ABBY *is clearly apprehensive—about* RAY, *not about anything
outside.*

ABBY: . . . So?

RAY: I think someone's watching.

ABBY *doesn't understand, and has had enough. As she throws
the light back on:*

ABBY: So what'll they see?

RAY turns angrily from the window.

RAY: Just leave it off. He can see in.

EXT   FACING ROOF

RAY and ABBY are once again clearly visible. RAY is starting across the room.

INT   ABBY'S APARTMENT

ABBY takes a fearful step back as RAY strides toward the light switch, next to her.

ABBY *(abruptly)*:   —If you do anything the neighbors'll hear.

This brings RAY up short. He stares at ABBY. It registers that it is him she's afraid of.

RAY: You think . . .

He shakes his head.

. . . Abby. I meant it . . . when I called . . .

ABBY takes another step back. Her voice comes out, after a pause, half-strangled:

ABBY: . . . I love you too.

RAY winces. He slowly shakes his head with a pained half-smile.

RAY: Because you're scared.

We hear the dull report of a rifle and the deafening sound of shattering glass. The gun shot hits RAY in the back, knocking him to the floor. He lies still.

CLOSE SHOT   ABBY

She stares dumbly down at RAY. She looks slowly up to the window.

THE WINDOW

It has a gaping black hole. The sound of shattering glass still reverberates in the apartment. Small shards of glass chink down from the window and shatter on the floor.

BACK TO ABBY

Staring at the window, paralyzed—almost in a trance. Quiet except for the chinking of glass.

EXT   FACING ROOF

We are looking through the telescopic sight of a high-powered rifle. The rifle sweeps up from RAY's body across the brightly lit room, and centers ABBY, still staring at the window, in the cross hairs.

INT   ABBY'S APARTMENT

We are looking past ABBY toward the shattered window at the far end of the room. A brass lamp stands in the foreground, between ABBY and the camera. ABBY still stands paralyzed.

Glass has stopped chinking from the window to the floor; there is a painful silence.

Suddenly ABBY dives to the floor just as CRASH the rest of the window falls away and PING the brass lamp somersaults toward us from the impact of the bullet.

The window is now completely gone—just a black hole in the brightly lit wall.

ABBY

Scrambles into a corner at the window end of the room. The only sound is her heavy breathing. She looks over at RAY, *then up at the bulb on the ceiling.*

ABBY'S POV   CEILING BULB
BACK TO ABBY

Breathing heavily, almost hysterical. She looks down at the floor.

ABBY'S POV

RAY *is sprawled on the floor in a pool of blood and broken glass.*

BACK TO ABBY

She reaches down and pulls off one of her shoes. She throws it at the ceiling bulb.
   We hear the bulb shatter and the room goes black.
   ABBY *rises and makes her way cautiously across the glass-littered floor toward* RAY. *She stoops over him.*

LOW SHOT   THE DARK APARTMENT

Its front door in the background. ABBY *rises into frame and backs toward the doorway, staring down at the floor. One of her hands is covered with blood.*

ABBY: Ray—

She winces and almost loses her balance as we hear a piece of glass crunching under her bare foot. She turns and moves to the front door, favoring one foot, and throws the door open.

HALLWAY

ABBY *lurches from her apartment and pounds on the neighboring door. No answer. She pounds on the door across the hall.*

OLD WOMAN'S VOICE (*frightened, in Spanish*):   Get away! I'll call my son-in-law!

ABBY (*groping for the words, in Spanish*):   No no—you don't understand—

OLD WOMAN'S VOICE (*in Spanish*):   He has a gun!

ABBY heads for the stairway at the far end of the hall. The heel of her shod foot is throwing her weight onto her bad foot; she kicks off the shoe.

CLOSE SHOT ABBY

As she reaches the top of the stairs. She takes one step down, then brings herself up short. She looks over the railing down the stairwell. It is quiet. An innocent-sounding cough echoes somewhere in the building.

We hear the sound of footsteps from somewhere below.

ABBY turns and hobbles back to her apartment. The bareness of the hallway sets off her abandoned shoe.

ABBY'S APARTMENT

As she enters and slams the door behind her. She scrabbles at the lock, finally manages to get it shut, then turns and looks frantically around.

ABBY'S POV

RAY is lying still in the darkness.

We can hear footsteps approaching up the hallway.

ABBY enters frame and kneels down next to RAY. She fumbles around him briefly in the darkness.

The doorknob rattles. ABBY freezes, listening, trying to control her breath. After a moment we hear a scraping at the lock.

ABBY moves to the bathroom adjoining the main room and shuts the door behind her.

BATHROOM

It is very small. ABBY presses her palms against the door and slowly eases her ear against the door to listen. The scraping in the apartment door lock continues. Sweat streams down ABBY's face. She brushes a drop from her eye.

We hear the snap of the lock springing open, and the front door swinging on its hinges.

CLOSER ON ABBY

Her ear pressed to the door. From the next room we hear the sound of footsteps crunching across broken glass.

ABBY backs away from the door, stares at it, then turns and moves to the bathroom window. She looks out.

ABBY'S POV

A sheer drop to the narrow backyard of the building four stories below. Next to ABBY's window is another window, separated from hers only by the breadth of the wall, that separates the two apartments.

ABBY'S APARTMENT

VISSER hunches, hands on knees, over RAY, who lies on the floor out of frame.

VISSER (*grimly*):   All right . . .

He hunkers down closer to RAY.

. . . You got some of my personal property.

He is rummaging through RAY's pockets but comes up empty-handed.

. . . One of you does.

VISSER looks down at RAY, glances around the room, looks back down at RAY.

. . . I don't know what the hell you two thought you were gonna pull.

His hand, gripping something, flashes down out of frame. We hear a dull crunch.

BATHROOM

ABBY *has drawn her head back from the bathroom window. She moves back to the door and braces herself against it.*

ABBY'S APARTMENT

VISSER *straightens up from* RAY's *body. He drops something to the floor, out of frame, that lands with a thud.*

He goes over to the light switch on the wall and flips it back and forth. No light.

He goes over to the brass lamp, sets it upright, tries its switch. Again nothing.

He disappears into the kitchenette as we hold on its open doorway. After a moment we hear a refrigerator hum as a cold blue light plays on the doorway. There is the rattle of a can being pulled off the refrigerator rack, and the snap of its pull-tab being opened. After a couple of audible slurps we hear the can go back on the rack and, as the blue light disappears, we hear the refrigerator door close.

VISSER *reappears in the doorway. He surveys the room, fixes on the bathroom door, goes over, turns the knob. The door swings open.*

He walks in.

BATHROOM

VISSER *looks around the cramped space. The shower curtain is drawn. He casually draws it back. The shower is empty.*

He goes to the window and leans out.

VISSER'S POV

The sheer drop below; the other window to one side.

BACK TO VISSER

He draws his head back in, presses his palms against the adjacent wall, and eases his ear to the wall to listen.

Perfect quiet.

After a moment he goes back to the window, braces himself against the sash, and sticks his arm out—groping for the window of the adjacent apartment.

EXT   ABBY'S BUILDING/BATHROOM WINDOW
CLOSE SHOT   VISSER'S FACE

Pressing against the glass as he leans against the upper half of the bathroom window.

CLOSE SHOT   VISSER'S HAND

It finds the adjacent window and starts to raise it.

BACK TO VISSER'S FACE

Again we see him through the window. His jaw is set as he gropes offscreen.

Suddenly his body jerks violently forward, his head smacking against the glass and cracking it.

QUICK CUT TO:
INT   ADJACENT APARTMENT
CLOSE SHOT   VISSER'S HAND

ABBY (out of frame) has grabbed it and now THUMP she slams the window down on his wrist, catching it between the window sash and sill.

Her other hand flashes across frame to THUNK pin VISSER's hand to the sill with RAY's knife.

QUICK CUT:
BACK TO VISSER

We hear the shatter of glass as the shock causes his head to break through the window. His hand is nailed into the apartment next door. He is in pain.

ADJACENT APARTMENT

ABBY *backs slowly from the window, staring at the hand.*
From the ground below we hear the faint and echoing sounds
of the shards of glass shattering against pavement.

ABBY'S POV   THE WINDOW

VISSER's *pinned hand is writhing.*
   As we hear a muffled CRACK, a circle of light opens with
a puff of plaster dust in the wall that separates the two
apartments. A line of light shoots across the dark apartment
from the bright bathroom next door.

BACK TO ABBY

Staring at the wall. We hear a second CRACK.

ABBY'S POV

A second small hole has opened in the wall, letting through a
second shaft of light.
   Four more sharp reports in rapid succession: With each
gun blast a bright circle opens and a new shaft of light
penetrates the dark apartment.
   Finally we hear the CLICK of an empty chamber, and the
clatter of the empty gun being dropped to the floor of the
bathroom next door.

CLOSE SHOT   ABBY

Staring at the lines of light that crisscross the apartment.
   There is a long moment of silence, then a sudden THUMP.

ABBY'S POV   THE WALL

Six circles of light.
   The circles go black momentarily as there is another
THUMP. And another. Each time VISSER *pounds his fist*
against the wall, there is a muffled THUMP and his
swinging arm strobes the bullet holes.

M. Emmet Walsh

BACK TO ABBY

She turns and hobbles toward the door of the apartment. The muffled thumping continues, as in her dream.

HALLWAY

As ABBY emerges from the adjacent apartment. She stops and looks down the hall.

ABBY'S POV

The stairway is at the far end of the hall. The door of her own darkened apartment stands slightly ajar.

ADJACENT APARTMENT
CLOSE SHOT   THE WALL

The bullet holes strobing. The pounding, more purposeful now, grows louder and more intense.

Finally, with a crash, VISSER's fist penetrates the wall in an explosion of light and dust.

HALLWAY

We pull ABBY as she limps hesitantly down the hall.

ADJACENT APARTMENT
CLOSE SHOT   VISSER'S HAND

Waving aimlessly through the ambient dust. He is blindly groping for the sill—and the knife that pins his other hand.

His outstretched middle finger just grazes the handle of the knife.

ABBY'S HALLWAY/APARTMENT

Pulling ABBY as she draws even with the door of her apartment.

ABBY'S POV

Her pearl-handled revolver sits on the shelf just inside the door, where RAY left it. It catches the light from the hall.

ADJACENT APARTMENT
EXTREME CLOSE SHOT   VISSER'S FINGERTIPS

The side of his middle finger rubs against the knife handle; the tip of his index finger barely touches it. VISSER's fingers are trembling, indicating that his arm is stretched to its uttermost.

A surge against the wall gives his fingers another inch or so and they curl around the handle of the knife.

ABBY'S APARTMENT
CLOSE SHOT   ABBY

As she steps in from the hallway to pick up the gun. She looks around the apartment.

ABBY'S POV

The window of the apartment, its glass now completely gone, lets in streetlight. RAY's corpse is a dark form in the middle of *the floor. A bright shaft of light slices across the room from offscreen. It glints on the shards of glass that litter the floor, just as in* ABBY'*s dream.*

BATHROOM
CLOSE SHOT   VISSER

As he slowly, quietly draws his hand in from the hole in the wall. He is holding the knife.
   He turns slowly to face the door, listening.

ABBY'S APARTMENT
CLOSE SHOT   ABBY

She steadies herself against the wall and turns to look toward the bathroom.

ABBY'S POV

The bathroom door stands slightly ajar. The interior of bathroom is a bright band in the shadowy recesses of the back of the apartment.

BATHROOM
CLOSE SHOT   VISSER

Moving quietly toward the door.

ABBY'S APARTMENT
CLOSE SHOT   ABBY

Staring, almost transfixed, at the bathroom door. She raises the gun, trembling, and trains it on the band of light.

ABBY'S POV

VISSER'*s shadow falls across the crack in the doorway.*

BACK TO ABBY

She shifts the gun slightly and fires.

Frances McDormand

ABBY'S POV

With the roar of the gun, a small circle of light opens in the door. As the door waffles under the impact, we hear VISSER *collapsing behind it.*

BACK TO ABBY

Leaning against the facing wall. She lowers the gun. She slides down the wall to finally rest seated on the floor. She brushes a drop of sweat from her eye.

HER POV

The cracked bathroom door spilling light.

BACK TO ABBY

A pause. After a moment, her voice comes out half-choked:

ABBY: . . . I ain't afraid of you, Marty.

HER POV

The bathroom door. Quiet for a long moment.
Then, from inside the bathroom, we hear laughter.

BACK TO ABBY

Staring at the door. We hear the laughter subside, to leave the sound of labored breathing. Finally:

VISSER (*os*):   . . . Well ma'am . . .

BATHROOM

VISSER *lies on his back, his head underneath the bathroom sink.*
His good hand is pressed against his belly, which rises and falls with his heavy breathing. Blood seeps out between his fingers.
He is smiling.

VISSER: . . . If I see him, I'll sure give him the message.

HIS POV

The underside of the sink, its convoluted chrome works beading moisture.

VISSER

Looking, with mild interest.

HIS POV

A condensed droplet trickles down the chrome.
   Directly overhead, it hangs for a moment from the lowest joint of the pipe.
   It fattens, wavers, wavers—and falls, spelling . . .

FINIS

Raising Arizona

Raising Arizona and *Evil Dead II:*

A Colloquium

In March of 1986 *Raising Arizona*, a feel-good movie about cute little babies, and *Evil Dead II: Dead by Dawn*, a feel-good splatter movie, had their commercial openings on the same day. In order to illuminate other similarities between the two pictures, Joel and Ethan Coen, the authors of the first movie, chatted with their friends Sam Raimi, Robert Tapert, and Bruce Campbell, respectively the director, producer, and star of the second.

Joel: We very much enjoyed *Evil Dead II: Dead by Dawn*.

Rob: Thank you.

Ethan: Our hats are off to you!

Bruce: Thanks. We enjoyed *Raising Arizona*.

Ethan: We congratulate you!

Sam: Thanks.

Ethan: You boys did a remarkable job. *Evil Dead II* is a great picture by anybody's—according to anyone you ask. Everyone says it's a great picture—and it is!

Bruce: Thank you, thanks a lot.

Joel: As you know, our picture just came out also, *Raising Arizona*—

Rob: And that was a great picture!

Joel: Uh-huh. And not just according to you, but according to lots of other people too. Throughout the entire industry, and the public at large.

Bruce: Well you deserve all the praise in the world for that picture.

Joel: Uh-huh.

Ethan: So *Evil Dead II*. How did you do it? How did—all the effects, the complicated camera stuff?

Sam: Actually it was—

Ethan: Was it a team effort?

Rob: You surround yourself with people who—

Joel: So you're saying, Yes, it was a team effort?

Rob: Okay, yeah—

Joel: Our picture was a team effort too. That aspect of it was highly praised. But do you want to know something?

Rob: Sure.

Joel: In our picture, the main couple, who live in a trailer—that trailer was all built on a sound stage. It was totally fake.

Sam: Yeah, well the cabin in our picture, where all the action takes place, we built that on a stage too.

Joel: Big deal, everyone does that.

Sam: Yeah—

Ethan: In the olden days, in Hollywood, almost all pictures were all shot inside on a stage and stuff. Also they had the star system and big producers like Irving J. Thalberg.

Bruce: Yeah, I know.

Joel: How do you respond when people accuse your pictures of being grand guignol?

Bruce: Well it's not a criticism, it's not a negative thing.

Joel: It is so. Don't you know what grand guignol is? They're not saying your picture is grand, like the Freddy pictures are just plain guignol but your pictures are *grand* guignol. It's all just one thing, grandguignol. It goes together.

Bruce: Yeah but it doesn't mean something bad or derogatory. It just means that they're sort of gory and fun.

Joel: It does?

Bruce: Yeah.

Ethan: Well congratulations on your achievement! We thought *Evil Dead II: Dead by Dawn* was a great picture. But do you want to know something? A lot of it was fakey. Like that scene where the dead woman danced around under her decapitated head? Totally fakey. That couldn't happen.

Rob: I think it's a question of fantasy. It's not supposed to be like real life.

Ethan: But you never said that! You never say that in the movie!

Joel: You never said it!

Sam: But people know, from the advertising and stuff, they know the kind of movie—

Bruce: What about *your* movie? You have a biker blow a lizard off a rock, from a moving motorcycle, from like 200 feet away—

Ethan: That's different.

Bruce: It's a movie!

Joel: That's different. That could happen. A guy on a motorcycle, if he's a good shot, plenty of practice and so forth, he could do that. Maybe not hit the lizard every time, but it's possible. We just had him do it once. If everything breaks the right way, it's possible. Whereas in your picture, the dancing around with no head, even if everything broke right, no.

Sam: It's a fantasy—

Joel: Well I guess that's as good a cop-out as any.

Ethan: What are the themes of your picture?

Sam: Well it doesn't really . . . it's just entertainment.

Ethan: Yeah, but what are the themes? Like ours, we

	had, family life versus being an outlaw. What was yours?
Rob:	I guess you could say good versus evil—Bruce's character, Ash, being good, against the forces of evil.
Ethan:	Sounds pretty heavy for an entertainment picture.
Bruce:	Well it was treated with a light touch.
Joel:	We treated ours with a light touch also. Many people have commented on that, in the many publications which ran big stories about our picture.
Ethan:	Do you like message pictures?
Rob:	I, uh . . . I like a picture with a good message.
Ethan:	Would you go to see a message picture or a Freddy picture? If they were both playing at the same time.
Joel:	If you could only see one.
Rob:	Well, like, what's the message picture?
Ethan:	*Guess Who's Coming to Dinner.*
Rob:	. . . God, I don't know.
Ethan:	How about a message picture or a really good meal?
Joel:	With all the trimmings.
Ethan:	Somebody else paying.
Rob:	I don't . . . I . . .
Ethan:	Sam, how about you?
Sam:	I don't . . . what would *you* pick?
Joel:	The message picture.
Ethan:	Congratulations again on *Evil Dead II: Dead by Dawn!*
Bruce:	Thanks—
Ethan:	We gotta go.
Joel:	We're interviewing Coppola.

Credits

The Players

H.I.	Nicolas Cage
Ed	Holly Hunter
Nathan Arizona Sr.	Trey Wilson
Gale	John Goodman
Evelle	William Forsythe
Glen	Sam McMurray
Dot	Frances McDormand
Leonard Smalls	Randall "Tex" Cobb
Nathan Junior	T. J. Kuhn
Florence Arizona	Lynne Dumin Kitei
Prison Counselor	Peter Benedek
Nice Old Grocery Man	Charles "Lew" Smith
Younger FBI Agent	Warren Keith
Older FBI Agent	Henry Kendrick
Ear-Bending Cellmate	Sidney Dawson
Parole Board Chairman	Richard Blake
Parole Board Members	Troy Nabors
	Mary Seibel
Hayseed in the Pickup	John O'Donnal
Whitey	Keith Jandacek
Minister	Warren Forsythe
"Trapped" Convict	Ruben Young
Policemen in Arizona House	Dennis Sullivan
	Dick Alexander
Feisty Hayseed	Rusty Lee
Fingerprint Technician	James Yeater

Credits

Reporters	Bill Andres
	Carver Barnes
Unpainted Secretary	Margaret H. McCormack
Newscaster	Bill Rocz
Payroll Cashier	Mary F. Glenn
Scamp with Squirt Gun	Jeremy Babendure
Adoption Agent	Bill Dobbins
Gynecologist	Ralph Norton
Mopping Convict	Henry Tank
Supermarket Manager	Frank Outlaw
Varsity Nathan Jr.	Todd Michael Rogers
Machine Shop Earbender	M. Emmet Walsh
Glen and Dot's Kids	Robert Gray
	Katie Thrasher
	Derek Russell
	Nicole Russell
	Zachary Sanders
	Noell Sanders
Arizona Quints	Cody Ranger
	Jeremy Arendt
	Ashley Hammon
	Crystal Hiller
	Olivia Hughes
	Emily Malin
	Melanie Malin
	Craig McLaughlin
	Adam Savageau
	Benjamin Savageau
	David Schneider
	Michael Stewart

and Featuring the Amazing Voice of William Preston Robertson

Directed by	Joel Coen
Produced by	Ethan Coen
Written by	Ethan Coen and Joel Coen
Co-Produced by	Mark Silverman
Executive Producer	James Jacks
Associate Producer	Deborah Reinisch
Director of Photography	Barry Sonnenfeld
Production Designer	Jane Musky

CREDITS

Edited by	Michael R. Miller
Music by	Carter Burwell
Costume Designer	Richard Hornung
Supervising Sound Editor	Skip Lievsay
Associate Editor	Arnold Glassman
Casting by	Donna Isaacson C.S.A.
	and John Lyons C.S.A.
Stunt Coordinator	Jery Hewitt
Stunt Players	Jery Hewitt
	Bill Anagnos
	Curt Bortel
	Shane Dixon
	Allan Graf
	Cindy Wills Hartline
	Gene Hartline
	Jeff Jensen
	Edgard Mourino
	Ron Nix
	Spanky Spangler
Production Manager	Kevin Dowd
Production Supervisor	Alma Kutruff
Production Auditor	Barbara-Ann Stein
First Asst. Directors	Deborah Reinisch
	Kelly Van Horn
Second Asst. Directors	Jon Kilik
	Patricia Doherty
	Chitra Mojtabai
Location Manager	David Pomier
Prod. Office Coordinators	Christopher Buchanan
	Sharon Roesler
Second Unit and Post-Prod. Manager	Andrew Sears
Assistant Auditor	Laura McGillicuddy
Camera Operator	David M. Dunlap
Assistant Camera	Richard P. Crudo
	C. Mitchell Amundsen
Camera Dept. Asst.	Brad S. Mudgett
Steadicam Operator	Stephen St. John
Prod. Still Photographer	Melinda Sue Gordon
Production Sound Mixer	Allan Byer
Boom Operator	Peter F. Kurland
Additional Boom	Randy Gable
Recordist	Greg Horn

Credits

Re-Recording Mixer	Mel Zelniker
Key Grip/Dolly Grip	Dennis Gamiello
Rigging Grip	John "Earl" Lowry
Best Boy Grip	Brian Fitzsimmons
Grips	Cindy Lagerstrom
	Bob Preston
	Marty Miller
	Tom Dreesen
Gaffer	Russell Engels
Best Boy	Kenneth R. Conners
First Electric	Michael Burke
Electricians	Bob Field
	George Ball
	Dan MacCallum
	Craig Woodruff
	Michael Hall
Art Director	Harold Thrasher
Set Decorator/Draftsperson	Robert Kracik
Key Set Dresser	Marcia Calosio-Foeldi
Set Dressers	Roger Belk
	Chris Russchon
	Linette Forbes Shorr
Construction Coord.	Stephen Roll
Lead Carpenter	Terry Kempf
Carpenters	Pasco Di Carlo
	Star Fields
	Bill Holmquist
	Bill Seifried
	Chuck Seifried
Scenic Artists	Mark Donnelly
	Todd Hatfield
Storyboard Artist	J. Todd Anderson
Make-up	Katharine James-Cosburn
Hair	Dan Frey
Asst. to Costume Designer	Ellen M. Ryba
Wardrobe Supervisor	Stephen M. Chudej
Wardrobe Assistants	Wendy Cracchiolo
	Ada Akaji
	Brian Kirk
Costume Construction	Mary Ann Ahern
Hair and Make-up Assistant	Camille Henderson

CREDITS

Property Master	Roger Pancake
Asst. Property Master	Jan Fead
Property Man	Britt Torney
Special Effects	Image Engineering, Inc.
Special Effects Coord.	Peter Chesney
Special Effects Lead	Guy Louthan
Animal Action by	Karl Lewis Miller
Arizona Casting	Sunny Seibel
Extras Casting	Becca Korby-Sullivan
Baby Casting	Yvonne Van Orden and Joseph Schneider, Inc., New York City
Baby Wrangler	Julie Asch
Dialect Coach	Julie Adams
Sound Editors	Philip Stockton
	Magdaline Volaitis
	Ron Bochar
First Asst. Editor	Michael Berenbaum
Asst. Editor	Kathie Weaver
Asst. Sound Editors	Bruce Pross
	Marissa Littlefield
	Steven Visscher
	Christopher Weir
Apprentice Editor	Brian Johnson
Script Supervisor	Thomas Johnston
A. D. Production Assts.	Maureen Hymers
	Erin Stewart
	Eric Tignini
Production Secretary	Valerie Susan Brown
Location Assistant	Adam Grad
Location Prod. Assts.	Rick Ashman
	Matt Cartsonis
	L. R. Kelly
	Kim Seeger
Art Dept. Assts.	John Anderson
	Flint Esquerra
	Robb Roetman
	Katie Tansley
	Gerry Thrasher
Office Assistant	Blake Hocevar
Craft Services	Bob Childers
	Elizabeth Boyd

Credits

Special Electronic Sound Effects	Frederick Szymanski
	Jun Mizumachi
	Carl Mandelbaum
Foley Artist	Marko A. Constanzo
Foley Engineer	Michael Barry
Dolby Consultant	Michael DiCosimo
Negative Cutting	J. G. Films, Inc.
Title design by	Dan Perri
Music Engineering	Sebastian Niessen
Banjo	Ben Freed
Jews Harp, Guitar	Mieczyslaw Litwinski
Yodeling	John R. Crowder
Digital Score Assistant	Dan Conte

Special thanks to:

Dick Bowers

Office of the Mayor and City Manager, City of Scottsdale, Arizona

Phoenix Motion Picture/Commercial Coordinating Office

Arizona Film Commission

Carol Porter

Short Stop Markets

A Cardon Company, Tempe, Arizona

Home Depot Stores

Golden Horseshoe Stables, Scottsdale, Arizona

Happy Valley Landscape Supply

Dom Masters

Kurt Woolner

Susan Rose

Indian Jewelry Courtesy of Gilbert Ortega Fine Indian Jewelry

Reata Pass Steak House, Scottsdale, Arizona

Señor Greaser

Dental Work Courtesy of Dr. Gary M. Johnson

Eyewear Courtesy of Dr. Berton Siegel, O.D.D.O.

John Raffo

Portions of this picture were filmed in the Tonto National Forest, Forest Service, U.S. Department of Agriculture

Lighting and Grip Equipment Supplied by GENERAL CAMERA WEST, Los Angeles

Lenses and Panaflex Camera by PANAVISION
Supplied by GENERAL CAMERA EAST, New York

Color by DuART

Post Production Services by SOUND ONE and THE SPERA CORPORATION

CREDITS

This picture was shot on location in Arizona's Valley of the Sun
  A Great Place to Raise Your Kids

OVER BLACK:

VOICE-OVER: My name is H. I. McDunnough . . .

A WALL

With horizontal hatch lines.

VOICE-OVER: . . . Call me Hi.

A disheveled young man in a gaily colored Hawaiian shirt is launched into frame by someone offscreen.
    He holds a printed paddle that reads "NO. 1468-6 NOV 29 79."
    The hatch marks on the wall behind him are apparently height markers.

VOICE-OVER: . . . The first time I met Ed was in the county lock-up in Tempe, Arizona . . .

FLASH

As his picture is taken.

CLOSE UP

On the paddle: "NOV 29 79."

VOICE-OVER: . . . a day I'll never forget.

A bellowing male voice from offscreen:

SHERIFF: Don't forget the profile, Ed!

ANGLE ON THE STILL CAMERA

It is mounted on a tripod. A pretty young woman in a severe police uniform peers out from behind it.

WOMAN: Turn to the right.

HI: What kind of name is Ed for a pretty thing like you?

ED: Short for Edwinna. Turn to the right!

HI obliges, but still looks at ED out of the corner of his eye.

HI: You're a flower, you are. Just a little desert flower.

FLASH

On his eye-skewed profile.

HI: Lemme know how those come out.

LOW ANGLE   CELL BLOCK CORRIDOR

As HI is escorted away from the camera toward his cell.
At the far end of the corridor a huge CON is sluggishly mopping the floor.

VOICE-OVER: I was in for writing hot checks which, when businessmen do it, is called an overdraft. I'm not complainin', mind you; just sayin' there ain't no pancake so thin it ain't got two sides. Now prison life is very structured—more than most people care for . . .

INTERCUTTING

HI's POV of the MOPPING CON, tracking as he approaches, and the MOPPING CON's POV of HI as HI approaches.

VO: . . . But there's a spirit of camaraderie that exists between the men, like you find only in combat maybe . . .

The MOPPING CON snarls as HI passes:

CON: Grrrr . . .

VO: . . . or on a pro ball club in the heat of a pennant drive.

NEWSREEL FOOTAGE

A ballplayer connects—THWOCK—for a home run and the crowd roars.

Nicolas Cage (Hi) in center

PRISON HALL

Panning a circle of men who sit facing each other in folding chairs. The pan starts on HI.

VO: In an effort to better ourselves we were forced to meet with a counselor who tried to help us figure out why we were the way we were . . .

At this point the pan has reached the COUNSELOR, an earnest, bearded young man who straddles a folding chair with his arms folded over its back.
He is addressing one of the cons:

COUNSELOR: Why do you use the word "trapped"?

CLOSE UP   BLACK CON

The huge muscle-bound black man with a shaved head is knitting his brow in consternation.

CON: Huh?

COUNSELOR: Why do you say you feel "trapped" . . . in a man's body?

CON: Oh . . .

He bites his lip, thinking; then, in a resonant bass voice:

. . . Well, sometimes I get the menstrual cramps real hard.

PAROLE MEETING ROOM

Three PAROLE OFFICERS—two men and a woman—face HI across a table.

CHAIRMAN: Have you learned anything, Hi?

HI: Yessir, you bet.

WOMAN: You wouldn't lie to us, would you Hi?

HI: No ma'am, hope to say.

CHAIRMAN: Okay then.

EXT 7-ELEVEN NIGHT

A beat-up Chevy pulls into the all-night store's empty parking lot.

VO: I tried to stand up and fly straight, but it wasn't easy with that sumbitch Reagan in the White House . . .

HI is getting out of the Chevy in a Hawaiian shirt, holding a pump-action shotgun.

. . . I dunno, they say he's a decent man, so . . .

He primes the shotgun—WHOOSH-CLACK—and heads for the store.

. . . maybe his advisers are confused.

FLASH

Full-face exposure of HI once again in front of the mug-shot wall.

ED: Turn to the right!

HI obliges but shoots sympathetic glances at ED who is obviously upset, wiping away tears and snuffling behind the camera.

HI: What's the matter, Ed?

ED: My fai-ants left me.

VO: She said her fiancé had run off with a student cosmetologist who knew how to ply her feminine wiles.

FLASH

On HI's profile. He turns back to ED.

HI: That sumbitch.

SHERIFF (*offscreen*):   Don't forget his phone call, Ed!

HI: You tell him I think he's a damn fool, Ed. You tell him *I* said so—H. I. McDunnough. And if he wants to discuss it he knows where to find me . . .

As another police officer starts to lead him away:

HI: . . . in the Munroe County Maximum Security Correctional Facility for Men . . .

CLOSE ON ED

Looking up through her tears as HI is led away.

HI (*os*):   . . . State Farm Road Number Thirty-one; Tempe, Arizona . . .

BACK TO HI

Struggling to call back over his shoulder as he is firmly led out the door.

HI: . . . I'll be waiting!

The door slams.

LOW ANGLE   CELL BLOCK CORRIDOR

As HI *is once again escorted toward his cell.*
  The MOPPING CON *is now in the middle-background, having worked his way about halfway up the corridor since last time we saw him.*

VO: I can't say I was happy to be back inside, but the flood of familiar sights, sounds and faces almost made it feel like a homecoming.

CLOSE ON MOPPING CON

As HI *passes.*

CON: Grrrr . . .

PRISON HALL

Group is meeting again.

COUNSELOR: Most men your age, Hi, are getting married and raising up a family. They wouldn't accept prison as a substitute.

HI *looks sheepish.*

COUNSELOR: . . . Would any of you men care to comment?

Two convicts sitting next to each other, GALE *and* EVELLE, *appear to be friends.*

GALE: But sometimes your career gotta come before family.

EVELLE: Work is what's kept *us* happy.

ANGRY BLACK CON: Yeah, but Doc Schwartz is sayin' you gotta accept responsibilities. I mean I'm proud to say *I* got a family . . . somewhere.

HIGH ANGLE   CELL

Looking down from the ceiling. In the foreground, lying on the top bunk, hands clasped behind his head as he stares off into space is MOSES. MOSES *is a gnarled, elderly black con with wire-rimmed spectacles.*

   On the lower bunk, also with hands clasped behind his head and staring off at the same spot in space, is HI.

VO: I tried to sort through what the Doc had said, but prison ain't the easiest place to think.

MOSES: An' when they was no meat we ate fowl. An' when they was no fowl we ate crawdad. An' when they was no crawdad to be foun', we ate san'.

HI: You ate what?

MOSES (*nodding*):   We ate san'.

HI: You ate sand?!

MOSES: Dass right . . .

PAROLE BOARD ROOM

HI faces the same three PAROLE OFFICERS *across the same table.*

CHAIRMAN: Well Hi, you done served your twenty munce, and seeing as you never use live ammo, we got no choice but to return you to society.

SECOND MAN: These doors goan swing wide.

HI: I didn't want to hurt anyone, sir.

SECOND MAN: Hi, we respect that.

CHAIRMAN: But you're just hurtin' yourself with this rambunctious behavior.

HI: I know that, sir.

CHAIRMAN: Okay then.

HIGH SHOT

Of a 7-Eleven parking lot, at night, deserted except for HI's car which sits untended, its engine rumbling.

VO: Now I don't know how you come down on the incarceration question . . .

HI backpedals into frame with a shotgun and a bag of cash.

. . . whether it's for rehabilitation or revenge . . .

He spins and grabs his car-door handle. Locked. He tries the back door. Locked.

. . . But I was beginning to think . . .

As we hear the wail of an approaching siren, HI takes it on the heel and toe.

. . . that revenge is the only argument makes any sense.

FLASH

On HI against the mug-shot wall.

ED: Turn to the right!

Holly Hunter (Ed)

SHERIFF (*os*):   Don't forget his latents, Ed!

CLOSE ON HI'S HAND

We see his right hand being efficiently manipulated by ED's
*two hands: She is rolling each of his inked fingers into the
appropriate space on an exemplar sheet.*

HI (*os*):   Hear about the paddy-wagon collided with the
see-ment mixer, Ed? . . . Twelve hardened criminals
excaped.

ED *titters offscreen.*

ED (*os*):   I heard that one.

*She is done rolling off his prints. Her hand lingers on top of
his.*
     HI's *other hand enters to rest on top of hers.*

HI (*os*):   Got a new beau?

ED (*os*):   No, Hi, I sure don't.

HI slips a ring off his own finger and slides it onto ED's.

HI (*os*):   Don't worry, I paid for it.

LOW ANGLE   CELL BLOCK CORRIDOR

The surly MOPPING CON has now worked his way up to the foreground.
   HI is being escorted past him to his cell.

VO: They say that absence makes the heart grow fonder, and for once they may be right.

Halfway up the corridor HI points casually at the floor.

HI: You missed a spot.

The MOPPING CON turns to watch him recede.

CON: Grrrr . . .

HIGH ANGLE   CELL

Same high shot with MOSES on the top bunk, HI on the lower.

VO: More and more my thoughts turned to Ed, and I finally felt the pain of imprisonment.

MOSES: An' momma would frow the live crawdad in a pot of boilin' water. Well one day I decided to make my own crawdad . . .

We begin to crane down to tighten on the absently staring HI.

. . . an' I frew it in a pot, forgettin' to put in the water, ya see . . .

MOSES' voice is mixing down as we lose him from frame.

. . . and it was like I was makin' popcorn, ya see . . .

VO: The joint is a lonely place after lock-up and lights out . . .

We are now very close on HI, staring.

. . . when the last of the cons has been swept away by the sandman.

HI'S POV

The underside of the top bunk.
  A sudden flash whitens and fades to leave the image of ED, smiling behind her camera, softly supered on the underside of the bunk.

BACK TO HI

He wearily turns his head to profile on the pillow and shuts his eyes.

VO: But I couldn't help thinking that a brighter future lay ahead—a future that was only eight to fourteen months away.

Eyes closed, he is illuminated by a flash.

PAROLE BOARD ROOM

HI and the same three officers.

CHAIRMAN: Got a name for people like you, Hi. That name is called recidivism.

SECOND MAN: Ree-peat O-fender.

CHAIRMAN: Not a pretty name, is it, Hi?

HI: No sir, it sure ain't. That's one bonehead name. But that ain't me anymore.

CHAIRMAN: You're not just tellin' us what we wanna hear?

HI: No sir, no way.

SECOND MAN: 'Cause we just wanna hear the truth.

HI: Well then I guess I *am* tellin' you what you wanna hear.

CHAIRMAN: Boy, didn't we just tell you not to do that?

HI: Yessir.

CHAIRMAN: Okay then.

TRACKING

Over HI's shoulder as he strides toward a door marked "Processing" and flings it open.
   It is the familiar booking room. ED looks up from her camera, having just snapped a picture of another suspect against the hatched wall.

HI: I'm walkin' in here on my knees, Ed—a free man proposin'.

HI cocks a finger at the suspect.

HI: Howdy Kurt.

ED'S ROOM

As she nervously frets at her white bridal gown in front of a mirror.

VO: And so it was.

SHERIFF (*os*):   Don't forget the boo-kay, Ed!

CLOSE SHOT   ED

Gazing earnestly into the camera. A congregation is seated behind her—the bride's side wearing police blues; the groom's side, Hawaiian shirts.

ED: I do.

CLOSE SHOT   HI

Also staring into the camera.

HI: You bet I do.

REVERSE

Over their shoulders, the minister.

MINISTER: Okay then.

FLASH

On the newlyweds smiling at the camera.

FLASH

On the newlyweds smiling at each other, profile to the camera.

HIGH WIDE SHOT   TRAILER PARK

In the middle of a vast expanse of desert.

VO: Ed's pa staked us to a starter home in suburban Tempe . . .

INT MACHINE SHOP

HI is working the drill press, wearing goggles and sweat-stained overalls.

VO: . . . and I got a job drilling holes in sheet metal.

Next to him idly stands BUD, a veteran of the shop, with a grimy face and a pair of goggles pushed up on his forehead.

BUD: So we was doin' paramedical work in affiliation with the state highway system—not actually practicin', y'understand—and me and Bill's patrollin' down Nine Mile—

HI: Bill Roberts?

BUD (*barking*):   No, not that motherscratcher! Bill Parker! Anyway, we're approachin' the wreck, and there's a spherical object a-restin' on the highway . . .

He pauses to blow and pop a bubble with his chewing gum.

. . . And it *don't* look like a piece a the car.

VO: Mostways the job was a lot like prison, except Ed was waitin' at the end of every day . . .

CASHIER'S WINDOW

HI is scowling at his paycheck. Behind the barred window a fat cashier grins.

VO: . . . and a paycheck at the end of every week.

CASHIER: Gummint do take a bite, don't she?

EXT   TRAILER

HI sits in a lawn chair in front of the trailer. ED sits on his lap, his arms around her.
   Both are wearing sunglasses, looking at the setting sun. The scene is suffused with a warm yellow light.

VO: These were the happy days, the salad days as they say . . .

As the sun sets, the light is turning from yellow to amber. HI and ED watch, their heads following its slow downward arc.

. . . and Ed felt that having a critter was the next logical step. It was all she thought about.

The amber is turning to a more neutral dusky light as the sun has set. HI and ED continue to stare at the point where it disappeared.

. . . Her point was that there was too much love and beauty for just the two of us . . .

The dusk is slipping away into darkness.

. . . and every day we kept a child out of the world was a day he might later regret having missed.

We are by now holding on pitch black. Crickets chirr. From the darkness:

ED: That was beautiful.

A CALENDAR

ED is crossing off the last day on the calendar before a day circled in red.

VO: So we worked at it on the days we calculated most likely to be fruitful . . .

INT   TRAILER

HI is wearily entering after a long day at work, clutching his lunchpail.

VO: . . . and we worked at it most other days just to be sure.

ED flies into frame and leaps into his arms, covering him with kisses.

TRAILER BEDROOM

In each other's arms, HI and ED roll over on the bed.

VO: Seemed like nothing could stand in our way now . . .

We pan with them rolling and continue off them to the night table, on which sits a framed pair of photographs of HI, probably taken by ED: One shows him full face, the other in profile.

EXT   TRAILER   TWILIGHT

ED sits in a lawn chair knitting a booty. HI stands in Bermuda shorts and an unbuttoned Hawaiian shirt, hosing down the minuscule patch of front lawn.

VO: . . . My lawless years were behind me; our child rearin' years lay ahead.

DUSTY ROAD LEADING UP TO TRAILER   DAY

A squad car, its siren wailing, kicks up dust as it roars into the foreground.

VO: And then the roof caved in.

HI approaches the driver's window as ED leans out sobbing.

ED: Hi, I'm barren.

CLOSE ON HI

Shock and disbelief.

VO: At first I didn't believe it, that this woman who looked as fertile as the Tennessee Valley could not bear children.

DOCTOR'S OFFICE

A doctor is pointing a pencil at various parts of a schematic picture of the female reproductive system, in a book which he holds open on the desk in front of him.

VO: . . . But the doctor explained that her insides were a rocky place where my seed could find no purchase.

REVERSE

On HI and ED seated on the other side of the desk. ED is weeping with grief and shame. HI, one arm draped over her shoulder, is staring dumbstruck at the picture.

VO: Ed was inconsolable.

CLOSE ON A FOLDER

The top sheet is from the Office of the Sheriff, Munroe County. The subject is H. I. McDunnough.

VO: We tried an adoption agency . . .

ADOPTION OFFICE

HI and ED are seated on folding chairs facing an agent's desk. HI wears a sport coat over his Hawaiian shirt. ED is in her dress blues.

HI: It's true I've had a checkered past, but Ed here is an officer of the law twice decorated . . .

THE AGENT

Looking, with a dead pan, from the file to HI.

HI: . . . So we figure it kind of evens out.

His face still deadly neutral, the agent looks back down at the file and unfolds the accordioned rap sheet, revealing it to be a couple feet long.

VO: . . . But biology and the prejudices of others conspired to keep us childless.

INT   SQUAD CAR

On ED as she stares vacantly out the passenger window.

VO: Our love for each other was stronger than ever . . .

ON HI

Driving. He looks from ED out to the road.

VO: . . . but I preminisced no return of the salad days.

TRAILER BATHROOM

Over HI's shoulder as he stares listlessly at himself in the mirror, a razor held forgotten in one hand, his face half lathered and half shaved.

VO: The pizzazz had gone out of our lives.

TRAILER BEDROOM

The bedroom is somewhat messy. ED *sits on the edge of the bed, also staring listlessly. Her police uniform is on but not yet buttoned. Her hands lie palm-up in her lap, like two dead fish.*

VO: Ed lost all interest in both criminal justice and housekeeping. Soon after, she tendered her badge.

MACHINE SHOP

Once again HI *works as his sweaty gum-chewing colleague stands idly by.*

VO: Even my job seemed as dry and bitter as a hot prairie wind.

BUD: So here comes Bill a-walkin' down Nine Mile— that's Bill Parker, y'understand—got his sandwich in one hand, the fuckin' head in the other . . .

ON HI DRIVING

Alone in his Chevy. He looks to the side.

VO: I even caught myself drivin' by convenience stores . . .

HIS MOVING POV

7-Eleven.

VO: . . . that weren't on the way home.

TRAILER LIVING ROOM

HI *and* ED *sit listlessly watching TV.*

vo: Then one day the biggest news hit the state since they built the Hoover Dam . . .

ED perks up, reacting to something on TV. HI notices her reaction and also sloughs off his stupor to watch.

. . . The Arizona quints was born.

THE TV

A newscaster silently reading copy. Behind him news footage of five nurses holding infants mortices in.

vo: By "Arizona" quints I mean they was born to a woman named Florence Arizona.

BACK TO HI AND ED

Watching intently. Eyes still locked on the set, ED reaches her hand out to HI. Eyes still locked on the set, HI takes her hand in his.

vo: As you probably guessed, Florence Arizona is the wife of Nathan Arizona. And Nathan Arizona—well hell, you know who he is . . .

THE TV   A LATE-NIGHT LOCAL COMMERCIAL

NATHAN ARIZONA, a stocky middle-aged man in a white polyester suit, is gesturing expansively with his white cowboy hat toward a one-story warehouse store with a football stadium parking lot, chroma-keyed in behind him.

NATHAN ARIZONA (*mixing up on the TV*):   So come on down to Unpainted Arizona for the finest selection in fixtures and appointments for your bathroom, bedroom, beaudoir!

VO: . . . The owner of the largest chain of unpainted furniture and bathroom fixture outlets throughout the Southwest.

NATHAN ARIZONA: And if you can find lower prices anywhere my name ain't Nathan Arizona!

BACK TO HI AND ED

As they slowly look from the TV set toward each other.

LINE OF NEWSPAPER VENDING MACHINES

HI lounges near one of the vending machines as a businessman puts in a quarter.

VO: Yep, Florence had been taking fertility pills, and she and Nathan had hit the jackpot.

The businessman takes his newspaper and releases the machine door as he turns to leave.
   HI snags the door before it closes and takes his own five-finger discount copy.
   He flips the paper over to look at the headline.

FRONT PAGE OF NEWSPAPER

The banner headline of the **Tempe Intelligencer** *is:*
ARIZONA QUINTS GO HOME! *The subhead: " 'More Than We Can Handle,' Laughs Dad." Next to it is a picture of* NATHAN.

VO: Now y'all who're without sin can cast the first stone . . .

A pull back from the paper shows HI and ED reading it together at home. They look from the paper to each other.
   HI opens to an inside page and we pan a row of pictures—the five tots with their names underneath: HARRY, BARRY, LARRY, GARRY *and* NATHAN JR.

. . . but we thought it was unfair that some should have so many while others should have so few.

BILLBOARD

In the middle of the desert. It reads: "WELCOME TO TEMPE! POPULATION 13,948 . . . PLUS FIVE!"

EXT TRAILER TWILIGHT

We are floating in toward ED who is seated, waiting, in the driver's seat of HI's Chevy. HI enters frame and cinches down a ladder that is tied to the roof of the car. Pieces of red flag flutter at either end of the ladder where it sticks out beyond the car.

VO: With the benefit of hindsight maybe it wasn't such a hot idea . . .

HI gets in the car.

FROM BEHIND THE CHEVY

It starts down the long, winding road leading away from the trailer, kicking up dust.

VO: . . . but at the time, Ed's little plan seemed like the solution to all our problems, and the answer to all our prayers.

The title of the film burns in: RAISING ARIZONA
   A building chord snaps off in a shock cut to:

SUBURBAN LIVING ROOM EVENING

Tableau of a couple at home. NATHAN ARIZONA is on the telephone, his stocking feet up on an ottoman. FLORENCE sits reading Dr. Spock's Baby and Child Care.
   The living room is dominated by a large oil portrait of NATHAN and FLORENCE, gazing out from the wall over the mantelpiece.

NATHAN (*into the phone*):   Eight hundred leaf tables and no chairs?! You can't sell leaf tables and no chairs! Chairs, you got a dinette set! No chairs, you got dick! I ask my wife she got more sense! . . .

A title is supered: THE ARIZONA HOUSEHOLD
From somewhere upstairs we hear an infant start to cry.
FLORENCE *stops reading and looks up at the ceiling.* NATHAN *is oblivious.*

NATHAN: . . . Miles, alls I know is I'm away from the office to have me some kids and everything goes straight to heck! I ain't gonna stand for it!

Another title is supered below the first: SEPTEMBER 17, 1985
The baby stops crying and FLORENCE*'s attention returns to her book.*

. . . Yeah, and if a frog had wings he wouldn't bump his ass a-hoppin'! I'm sick of your excuses, Miles! It is now . . .

As he throws out his wrist to look at his watch a third title is supered beneath the first two: 8:45 P.M.

. . . 8:45 in the P.M. I'm gonna be down to the store in exactly twelve hours to kick me some butt!

He starts to replace the receiver but brings it back with an afterthought:

. . . Or my name ain't Nathan Arizona!

As he slams the phone into the cradle the titles disappear.
Another baby starts crying. FLORENCE *looks up at the ceiling.*

NATHAN: That sounds like Larry.

NURSERY

Close on the crying baby as HI *bounces it, gently but desperately.*

HI: Shhhh! Shh! Nice baby . . .

He starts to lower it back into the crib. The crib is unpainted with the name of each baby burned Bonanza-style into the headboard: Harry, Barry, Larry, Garry, and Nathan Jr.
Instead of quieting as he is lowered into the crib, the squalling baby only sets off one of his brothers. HI *hurriedly lifts him back out.*
He looks desperately around the room.
The room is wallpapered with nursery rhyme characters. There are toys strewn around. There is one adult-sized easy chair in the corner.
HI *carries the baby over to the chair, stepping on and reacting to the squeal of a squeeze-me toy on the way. He sits the baby deep in the chair and then returns to the crib to deal with the second crying baby.*
He lifts the baby out of the crib and gently bounces it. This baby stops crying.
Another one in the crib starts bawling.
HI *sets the second baby down on the floor and gives it a rattle to keep it pacified. He reaches for the third baby in the crib. Sweat stands out on* HI's *brow. He is desperately chucking the third baby under the chin when we hear a muffled pthump!*
He whirls to look across the darkened room.
The first baby has dropped off the easy chair and is energetically crawling away toward a shadowy corner.

LIVING ROOM

NATHAN *and* FLORENCE *are sitting stock-still, staring at the ceiling. After a moment, another baby starts crying.*

Nicolas Cage

NATHAN: What're they, playing telephone?

They stare at the ceiling.

NURSERY

Loose babies are crawling everywhere.

  HI *is skittering across the room in a half-crouch, a baby
tucked under one arm, reaching out with the other as he
pursues a crawling baby across the room.*

  *He hefts the other baby with his free arm and brings the
pair back to the crib.*

  He turns to look frantically around the room.

  The other three babies have disappeared.

  There is perfect quiet.

  HI *goes over to the closet door, which is ajar, and swings it
open.*

  *He reaches under a moving pile of clothes on the floor and
pulls out a baby.*

  He returns it to the crib and freezes, listening.

The sound of a rattle.
He drops to the floor to look under the crib.

WIDE ANGLE   UNDER CRIB

A baby holding a rattle leers into the camera in the
foreground. Behind him HI, *on his stomach, is reaching in to*
grab at his leg.

HI *is pulling the baby out, away from the camera, when*
with a plop! a baby drops onto HI's *back from the crib above.*

HI *twists one arm back to grope for the baby crawling on*
top of him.

He is straightening up, a baby in each arm, when he reacts
in horror to something he sees across the room.

HIS POV

The hindquarters of a diapered baby are just disappearing
around the corner of the nursery door into the hallway.

LIVING ROOM

FLORENCE *and* NATHAN *are staring at the ceiling. After a*
beat we hear a muffled plop! on the ceiling. A beat later, the
bleat of the squeeze-me toy.

NATHAN: . . . Whyn't you go up and check on 'em?
They sound restless.

UPSTAIRS HALLWAY

The floor-level wide-angle shot shows a baby crawling toward
the camera in the foreground. Behind him, in the background,
just rounding the open door from the nursery, yet another
baby is making a mad dash for freedom.

HI *emerges from the nursery and, stepping around the*
background baby, trots toward the baby in the foreground. By
the time he reaches it the low-angle cropping shows us only
his feet and calves.

CLOSE ON HI

Perspiring as he tiptoes the last two steps to the baby.

HIS POV

The baby and, beyond it, the stairway down to the main floor. We hear footsteps approaching.

BACK TO HI

He scoops up the baby and hurriedly tiptoes away toward the nursery.

LOW-ANGLE REVERSE

The baby at the nursery door in the foreground; the staircase in the background. As HI reaches the baby we hear footsteps climbing the stairs.

HI's free arm comes down into frame to scoop the baby up and out of frame just as:

FLORENCE's head appears, bobbing up as she climbs the stairs.

She approaches the nursery, still clutching the Dr. Spock book.

NURSERY

As FLORENCE enters from the hallway door.

We track back into the room, on her, as she approaches the crib. Halfway there she freezes, staring, in shock.

HER POV

All of the babies have been replaced in the crib but not lying down: They are seated in a row, staring back at her, lined up against the far crib railing, like a small but distinguished panel on "Meet the Press."

THROUGH THE WINDSHIELD OF THE CHEVY

ED's point of view of HI approaching the car. He is shrugging and displaying a pair of manifestly empty hands.

CLOSE ON ED

Barely able to fight down her anger. Hissing:

ED: What's the matter?!

HI appears at her—the driver's—window.

HI: Sorry honey, it just didn't work out.

He is reaching to open the door but she slaps his hand away from the handle.

ED: What d'you mean it didn't work out?!

HI: They started cryin', then they were all over me . . .

He is trying to open the door, which ED is holding shut with all her might.

    . . . It was kinda horrifying—Lemme in, honey.

ED: Course they cried! Babies cry!

HI: I know that now! Come on honey, we better leave—

ED is rolling up the window and locking the door.

ED: You go right back up there and get me a toddler! I need a baby, Hi; they got more'n they can handle!

Muffled, through the closed window, and very forlorn:

HI: Aw honey I—

ED: Don't you come back here without a baby!

NURSERY

FLORENCE is holding one of the babies cradled against her shoulder. She is facing the hallway door; her back is to the crib and window. The baby, peeping out over her shoulder, is facing the window.

CLOSE ON BABY

Looking.

BABY'S POV

Of the window, as HI's head appears in it.

BABY

Looking.

HI

Looking back, he holds a finger to his lips.

BABY

FLORENCE starts bouncing it, patting it on the back.

BABY'S POV

HI and the window bouncing up and down.

LIVING ROOM

NATHAN is leafing through the lingerie ads in the newspaper. We can hear FLORENCE's returning footsteps. Muttering:

NATHAN: Christian Dior my butt . . .

FLORENCE enters.

. . . They pay money for that?

FLORENCE: Yes dear.

NATHAN: How're the kids?

FLORENCE: Fine dear.

NATHAN: Fuckin' kids, I love 'em.

We hear the bleat of the squeeze-me toy. FLORENCE *and* NATHAN *look at the ceiling for a beat, then* NATHAN *clears his throat and returns to the newspaper.*

CHEVY

ED *sits anxiously waiting in the driver's seat, peering intently through the windshield. As she catches sight of something she breaks into a broad smile, unlocks the door, and slides over to the passenger seat.*

HI *is opening the door with one hand, cradling a baby in the other.*

ED: Which one ya get?

As he gets into the driver's seat:

HI: I dunno. Nathan Jr., I think.

ED: Gimme here.

He hands her the infant, then hands her the copy of Dr. Spock's Baby and Child Care.

HI: Here's the instructions.

ED: Oh, he's beautiful!

HI *nods as he pulls away from the curb.*

HI: He's awful damn good. I think I got the best one.

ED is gushing and kissing the baby through the rest of the conversation.

ED: I bet they were all beautiful. All babies are beautiful!

HI: Yeah. This one's awful damn good though.

ED: Don't you cuss around him.

HI: He's fine, he is. I think it's Nathan Jr.

ED: We are doin' the right thing, aren't we Hi?—I mean, they had more'n they could handle.

HI: Well now honey we been over this and over this. There's what's right and there's what's right, and never the twain shall meet.

ED: But you don't think his momma'll be upset? I mean overly?

HI: Well a course she'll be upset, sugar, but she'll get over it. She's got four little babies almost as good as this one. It's like when I was robbin' convenience stores—

ED suddenly bursts out crying.

ED: I love him so much!

HI: I know you do, honey.

ED *(still sobbing)*:   I love him so much!

TRAILER LIVING ROOM

As the lights are thrown on. The room is hung with streamers. A string of cut-out letters reads "Welcome Home Son!"

HI (*os*):   Okay, bring him in!

REVERSE

ED is entering with NATHAN JR.

HI: This is it young Nathan Jr. Just feast your eyes about, old boy!

ED: Don't be so loud around him, Hi.

HI: (*softly*):   Damn, I'm sorry honey.

ED: And don't you cuss around him.

HI: Aw, he don't know a cuss word from shinola.

ED: Well see that he don't.

HI (*jovially*):   He's all right, he is.

He reaches for the child.

. . . Come on over here, Nathan Jr., I'll show you around.

He takes the baby in both hands and holds him out at arm's length, pointing him at the various places of interest. The baby looks google-eyed at each one.

. . . Lookahere, young sportsman. That-there's the kitchen area where Ma and Pa chow down. Over there's the TV, two hours a day maximum, either educational or football so's you don't ruin your appreciation of the finer things. This-here's the divan, for socializin' and relaxin' with the family unit. Yessir, many's the day we sat there and said wouldn't it be nice to have a youngster here to share our thoughts and feelin's—

Impatient with the nonsense:

ED: He's tired, Hi.

HI: Well we'll just sit you right there, boy . . .

He is propping NATHAN JR. *up in the corner of the couch.* HI *sits at the other corner and* ED *sits in a facing chair.*

. . . Just put those dogs up'n take a load off.

HI *beams at* NATHAN JR. ED *smiles at* NATHAN JR. NATHAN JR. *looks from one to the other, deadpan. They seem to be waiting for him to contribute to the conversation.*
    Silence.
    Suddenly HI *slaps his knee.*

HI: What are you kiddin'?! We got a family here!

ED *is getting up.*

. . . He's a scandal, honey! He's a little outlaw!

As she picks up the baby:

ED: He's a good boy.

HI: He ain't *too* good! You can tell by that twinkle in his eye!

ED: Don't you think we should put him to bed?

HI:　Hang on, honey . . .

He is frantically reaching for a Polaroid camera.

. . . Let's us preserve the moment in pictures!

ED:　Just one, okay? . . .

She sits down on the couch with NATHAN JR. *as* HI *starts screwing the camera into a tripod.*

. . . I gotta tell ya, I'm a little scared Hi.

Absently, as he sets up the camera:

HI:　How come is that, honey?

ED:　Well we got a baby, Hi. It's an awful big responsibility.

As he peers through the lens:

HI:　Honey, could ya slide over a tad and raise the nipper up?

As she complies:

ED:　I mean we never done this before and I'm kinda nervous.

HI:　You're doin' real good, sugar.

HI *sits on the couch, holding the camera's cable release. He puts his arm around* ED *and smiles at the offscreen camera.* ED *nestles her head against* HI's *shoulder.*

ED:　I love you, Hi.

HI: We're set to pop here, honey.

ED: You're gonna help, aren't ya?

Through his teeth as he continues to grin at the offscreen camera:

HI: How's that, honey?

ED: Give Nathan Jr. a normal family background, just quiet evenings at home together . . .

We begin to hear distant thunder.

HI: You can count on it, honey.

ED: . . . Everything decent'n normal from here on out.

HI: Uh-huh.

As he squeezes the cable release—FLASH—the image momentarily freezes on HI beaming, NATHAN JR. staring, and ED looking at HI with a little bit of concern.

DARK FIELD   SAME NIGHT

The rolling thunder has built to a thunderclap at the cut, and the flash of the Polaroid match cuts to lightning throwing a momentarily harsh glare on the field.

Rain beats down on the bare patch of ground we are looking at—by now just a patch of mud.

Faraway lightning flickers and we hear the rumble of more thunder approaching, then suddenly:

THWAK—a head pops up out of the mud. It is GALE, the con we saw in group therapy. He bellows as lightning and thunder flash and crack nearby.

His head is covered with mud, although the driving rain is already starting to wash it away.

We are beginning to track in an arc around GALE's head,
who is now struggling, working to get his shoulders and
arms up out of the mud. The end of the 180-degree arc and a
flash of lightning reveal, way in the distance, the wire-topped
walls of a penitentiary.

Still bellowing, as if in some primal rage, GALE has gotten
his muck-covered arms up out of the earth and is now
pushing down to haul up the rest of his body. It comes with
much effort, and with the loud sucking-popping sounds of the
fiercely clinging mud.

Finally he is free.

With a great cry, the mud-covered man plunges his right
arm straight back down into the earth, all the way up to his
shoulder. He gropes intently and then, apparently having
grabbed hold of something underground, he starts pulling.

His arm comes slowly back up out of the mud. Clasped in
his hand is—a human foot.

Bellowing with effort he continues to pull, liberating the
foot . . . leg . . . torso of his companion, and finally his head.

As the rain starts to wash the mud off his companion's
head we see that it is his friend EVELLE.

Both are bellowing.

Mud sucks and pops.

Thunder crashes.

INT   GAS STATION MEN'S ROOM

At the cut the ear-splitting thunder drops out to quiet. We
hear only the muffled patter of rain and the hum of a bare
fluorescent.

The two bedraggled escaped cons are standing side by side,
combing their hair in the mirror. The men seem absorbed in
their task, using hair jelly from a jar that sits on the shelf
between them to restore their duck's-ass haircuts.

EVELLE cracks the bathroom door and looks out into the
rain.

EVELLE: . . . Okay.

GALE: What is it?

EVELLE: Mercury. Looks nice.

EXT   GAS STATION

The two men are trotting out to a Mercury that sits untended at a gas island, a gas hose on automatic stuck in its tank.

As GALE *starts up the car* EVELLE *yanks the hose out and drops it to the ground.* GALE *is already starting to peel out as* EVELLE *gets in.*

WIDE SHOT   TRAILER LIVING ROOM

Late at night. HI *sits asleep on the sofa at the far end of the room, in a pool of lamp light.*

We hear faint, distant knocking. As we track in toward HI *the knocking becomes louder and more present.*

As we approach HI *we see that several Polaroids are spread over his gently rising and falling chest.*

By the time we tighten on his face the knocking has become quite loud.

VOICE: Open up!

HI *starts awake with a grunt.*

. . . Open up in air!

He looks up, alarmed.

HIS POV

The front door of the trailer. Someone is pounding insistently.

VOICE: Open up! It's a po-lice!

BACK TO HI

He sits up and tenses. He looks around.
ED stands in her nightgown at the mouth of the hallway, holding NATHAN JR. and squinting at HI. She hisses:

ED: Hi! What's goin' on?

VOICE: Po-lice, son! Open her up!

HI gets to his feet, hurriedly tosses the Polaroids under a cushion of the couch and takes out a gun.

HI: Get in the bedroom.

ED: They ain't gonna take Nathan?!

HI: Well I'd like to see 'em try.

As ED turns back to the bedroom:

VOICE: Open up and maybe we'll letcha plea-bargain.

BEDROOM

As ED enters and shuts the door. She listens hard at the door: HI's footsteps cross the living room, the click of the door opening, silence . . . a burst of raucous male laughter.

HI'S VOICE: . . . Honey! Come on out here! Want you to meet a couple friends of mine!

LIVING ROOM

As ED enters, carrying NATHAN JR. All three men—HI, GALE, and EVELLE—are beaming at her.

HI: Honey, like you to meet Gale and Evelle Snopes, fine a pair as ever broke and entered.

GALE *roars with laughter.*

. . . Boys, this-here's my wife.

GALE: Ma'am.

EVELLE: Miz McDunnough.

ED *smiles politely, then squints at* HI.

ED: Kind of late for visitors, isn't it Hi?

HI: Well yeah honey, but these boys tell me they just got outta the joint. Gotta show a little hospitality.

GALE *is admiring the baby.*

GALE: Well now H.I., looks like you been up to the devil's bidnis!

EVELLE: That a him or a her?

ED: It's a little boy.

GALE: Got a name, does he?

HI *and* ED *look at each other uncomfortably.* HI *clears his throat.*

HI: Well so far we just been using Junior.

ED: We call him Junior.

EVELLE: Say, that's good—J.R., just like on the Teevee.

GALE *is staring at the streamers and decorations. Reading aloud:*

GALE: "Welcome . . . Home . . . Son." Where's he been?

HI and ED respond simultaneously:

HI: Tulsa.

ED: Phoenix.

HI: He was, uh . . . he was visiting his grandparents.

ED: They're separated.

GALE: Was that yer folks ma'am?

ED: No, I'm afraid not.

GALE: I thought yer folks was dead, H.I.?

HI (*very uncomfortably*): Well we thought Junior should see their final resting place—Whyn't you boys have a seat?

As the two men move toward the couch ED hesitantly pipes up:

ED: Hi, it's two in the morning . . .

She wrinkles her nose.

. . . What's that smell?

Apologetically:

GALE: We don't always smell like this, Miz McDunnough. I was just explainin' to yer better half here that when we were tunnelin' out we hit the main sewer—dumb luck, that—and just followed that to—

ED: You mean you *busted* out of jail?!

GALE: Waaaal . . .

EVELLE: We released ourselves on our own recognizance.

GALE: What Evelle means to say is, we felt the institution no longer had anything to offer us . . .

He is looking at the baby.

. . . My Lord he's cute.

EVELLE: He's a little outlaw, you can see that.

ED: Now listen, you folks can't stay here!

GALE, EVELLE, and HI look up at ED, dumbstruck. After a beat:

EVELLE: . . . Ma'am?

ED: You just can't stay! I appreciate your bein' friends of Hi and all, but this is a decent family now . . .

She looks at HI.

. . . I mean we got a toddler here!

GALE leans in close to HI, a look of sincere concern on his face, and says under his breath:

GALE: Say, who wears the pants round here H.I.?

HI: Now honey—

ED: Don't you honey me. Now you boys can set a while and catch up, and then you'll be on your way.

There is an awkward silence as she leaves and slams the bedroom door.
   GALE is carefully studying his thumbnail; EVELLE stares fixedly at the ceiling. Still looking at his thumb:

GALE: Gotcha on a awful short leash, don't she H.I.?

BEDROOM

Sometime later, as HI tiptoes in. ED lies in bed facing the wall; we see only the back of her head. HI sits gingerly on the edge of the bed and, smiling, sticks a finger through the bars of the crib to play with the baby.
   The sound of the TV set in the living room filters faintly in.

ED: They still here?

HI is momentarily startled, then goes on playing with the baby.

HI: Yeah, they're just gonna stay a day or two. It's raining out honey, they got nowhere to go.

ED finally turns to face him. We hear the two men laugh raucously in the living room.

ED: They're fugitives, Hi . . .

HI turns to face her.

 . . . How're we gonna start a new life with them around?

HI: Well now honey you gotta have a little charity. Ya know, in Arab lands they'd set out a plate—

ED: Promise just a day or two.

HI: Tonight and tomorrow, tops.

EXTREME HIGH ANGLE

Looking straight down at HI, asleep in bed. It is later: filtering softly in from the other room is the end of the "Star Spangled Banner" on TV. We are craning down.

VO: That night I had a dream . . .

FLASH CUT

For a brief moment we see a wall of flames and hear it roar.

BACK TO HI

Still craning down.

VO: . . . I'd drifted off thinkin' about happiness, birth, and new life . . .

FLASH CUT

Wall of flames. Deafening roar.

BACK TO HI

Craning down. The faint National Anthem ends: we hear the WEEEEEEEE of a test pattern.

VO: . . . but now I was haunted by a vision of—

WALL OF FLAMES

Roaring. At the cut: WHOOOOOSH! a huge low-rider motorcycle bursts through the flames, its engine roaring even louder than the fire. Its driver is a huge leather-clad hellion. The chains worn by the BIKER *clank ominously as he rides.*

VO: He was horrible . . .

The BIKER *roars out of frame.*

LOW-ANGLE REVERSE

As the BIKER *roars into frame, his rear tire laying down a wake of fire.*

VO: . . . a lone biker of the apocalypse . . .

TRACKING ON BIKER

As he roars along a ribbon of desert highway.

VO: . . . a man with all the powers of hell at his command.

The BIKER *reaches for his bullwhip.*

. . . He could turn the day into night . . .

The BIKER *cracks the whip and, at the crack: The sky behind him turns instantly to black. Bolts of lightning crackle across it as thunder roars.*

ANOTHER DESERT SCENE   DAY

Tracking with and also in on the BIKER *from behind as he roars along a strip of highway. He is reaching for the two sawed-off shotguns which are strapped crisscross across his back.*

VO: . . . and laid to waste everything in his path.

REVERSE TRACK ON BIKER

Pulling the BIKER *from a distance as he levels the two shotguns. The tracking camera pulls back further to reveal a running jack-rabbit keeping pace with us in the foreground.*

VO:　　He was especially hard on the little things . . .

CRACK—as the first shotgun spurts orange the foreground rabbit keels over. The BIKER *slues the other gun around.*

LOCKED-DOWN WIDE SHOT

On a rock in the foreground, a desert lizard suns himself. The BIKER *is approaching in the distant background.*

VO:　　. . . the helpless and the gentle creatures.

CRACK—from afar, the foreground lizard is blown away.

LOCKED-DOWN LOW-ANGLE WIDE SHOT

*Of the empty desert road stretching away. In the foreground a lone desert flower blooms.
The* BIKER *roars into frame.*

VO:　　He left a scorched earth in his wake, befouling even the sweet desert breeze that whipped across his brow.

As the BIKER *roars away, the foreground flower bends with his draft and then bursts into flame.*

TRACKING ON BIKER

From in front. He twirls the shotguns in either hand and reaches back to plunge them over his shoulders into their holsters.

VO:　　I didn't know where he came from or why . . .

*We are moving in on his chest, where two crisscrossed
bandoliers carry two rows of hand grenades, their silver pins
glinting in the sun. We follow the line of one of the bandoliers
up to his right shoulder which bears the tattoo: "Mama
Didn't Love Me."*

. . . I didn't know if he was dream or vision . . .

REVERSE TRACK ON BIKER

*From behind, booming down as we track. We are approaching
the crest of a rise.*

VO: But I feared that I myself had unleashed him . . .

HIGH SHOT

Of the BIKER *approaching, craning down as he draws near.*

VO: . . . for he was The Fury That Would Be . . .

*With the crane down we momentarily lose him from view
over the rise; then suddenly—ROAR—he tops the rise and,
wheels spinning, is airborn.*

REVERSE

*As he crashes back down to earth in the foreground and roars
away. Only now we are no longer in the desert: We are
looking down a twilit street at the end of which is the Arizona
house.*

VO: . . . as soon as Florence Arizona found her little
Nathan gone.

*The roar of his engine and clank of his chains recede as the
BIKER gradually dissolves into thin air.
   We are left looking at the empty street and the faraway
Arizona house.
   The receding roar has left behind eerily beautiful singing, a*

woman singing a lullaby. Faintly, behind the singing, there is also a droning high-pitched noise.

The camera starts floating forward very close to the ground, moving slowly toward the Arizona house. The high-pitched drone is becoming less faint under the singing.

The camera is accelerating. The drone is growing louder— we can now tell that it is a human scream.

As we approach the Arizona house we can see that a ladder is propped up to a second-story window.

We are moving quite fast now. The scream all but buries the singing.

We are rushing toward the house, toward the base of the ladder, the sustained scream drawing us on.

We hurtle toward and then straight up the ladder with no abatement of speed, sucked forward by the deafening scream.

We reach the top and hurtle—THWAP!—through the white curtains of the open second-story window into the nursery to reveal FLORENCE ARIZONA, *her back to us, screaming over the crib.*

We are rocketing toward her.

She is turning to us, hands pressed to her ears, mouth stretched wide in an ear-splitting shriek and we are rushing into an extreme close-up of her gaping mouth and her wildly vibrating epiglottis and we

CUT TO:

EXTREME CLOSE SHOT   HI'S EYES

As they snap open.

The screaming snaps off at the cut. The singing that the building scream covered, however, is now audible again.

Perspiration beads HI's *forehead. He looks down toward the foot of the bed.*

THE BEDROOM

It is now morning. ED *walks back and forth, gently bouncing the baby as she walks. She is singing it a lullaby.*

Faintly, from the next room, we can hear GALE *and* EVELLE *snoring away like buzz saws.*

HI (*groggily*):   He all right?

ED: He's all right. He was just havin' a nightmare.

HI *is getting out of bed.*

HI: Yeah, well . . .

He crosses to the bedroom window and cracks the venetian blind. Orange light filters in.

HIS POV

Beyond a clothes line and a septic tank, a huge orange ball of sun is rising. We can almost hear the roar of its burning surface.

BACK TO HI

Looking.

HI: . . . Sometimes it's a hard world for little things.

HIS POV

The orange sun, rumbling, perceptibly rising.

ARIZONA HOME   FRONT FOYER

At the cut the rumble of the sun is snapped off by the high-pitched ba-WEEEEeeee . . . of a strobe going off as a flash picture is taken: We are looking over NATHAN SR.'s *shoulder as he stands at his open front door, facing a battery of press people who stand out on the porch.*

An obie light over a local TV news camera glares in at us; various flashbulbs pop.

NATHAN: —No, the missus and the rest of the kids've left town to I ain't sayin' where. They'll be back here when we're a nuclear fam'ly again.

VOICE: Mr. Arizona, which tot was abducted?

NATHAN: Nathan Jr., I think.

VOICE: Do you have anything to say to the kidnappers?

NATHAN: Yeah: Watch yer butt.

VOICE: Sir, it's been rumored that your son was abducted by UFOs. Would you care to comment?

NATHAN (*sadly*):   Now don't print that, son. If his mama reads that she's just gonna lose all hope.

A POLICEMAN *from inside the house is taking* NATHAN *by the elbow.*

POLICEMAN: We really have to ask you some more questions, sir . . .

As NATHAN *allows himself to be led back into the house he calls back over his shoulder:*

NATHAN: But remember, it's still business as usual at Unpainted Arizona, and if you can find lower prices anywhere my name still ain't Nathan Arizona!

We are following the two, hand-held, as the POLICEMAN *leads* NATHAN *toward the living room.*

LIVING ROOM

The room is filled with policemen milling about in several different uniforms: local police, state troopers, plainclothes detectives.

The original POLICEMAN *is leading* NATHAN *to a table where a white-smocked technician is preparing inkpad and exemplar sheets.*

The dialogue is urgent, rapid-fire and overlapping.

POLICEMAN: Mr. Byrum here can take your exemplars while you talk.

MR. BYRUM *has taken* NATHAN's *right hand and is rolling its fingers onto the inkpad.*

BYRUM: Just let your hand relax; I'll do the work.

NATHAN *jerks his hand away.*

NATHAN: What is this?! I didn't steal the damn kid!

Two men in conservative suits are approaching.

POLICEMAN: Sir, these men are from the FBI—

NATHAN (*bewildered*):   Are you boys crazy?! Alls I know is I wake up this morning with my wife screaming—

BYRUM (*patiently*):   We just need to distinguish your prints from the perpetrators', if they left any.

Giving his hand back:

NATHAN: Course! I know that!

FBI 1:   Sir, we have an indication you were born Nathan Huffhines; is this correct?

NATHAN: Yeah, I changed m'name; what of it?

FBI 2:   Could you give us an indication why?

NATHAN: Yeah, would you buy furniture at a store called Unpainted Huffhines?

FBI 1:   All right, I'll get to the point—

UNIFORMED COP: Was the child wearing anything when he was abducted?

NATHAN: No one sleeps nekkid in this house, boy! He was wear—

FBI 1:   I'm asking the questions here, officer.

COP: If we're gonna put out an APB we need a description of the—

NATHAN: He was wearin' his—

FBI 2:   It's just that we're better trained to intervene in crisis situations (*to* NATHAN). What was he wearing?

NATHAN: A dinner jacket! Wuddya think, he was wearing his damn jammies!

FBI 2 (*to* COP):   The child was wearing his jammies. Are you happy?

FBI 1:   Do you have any disgruntled employees?

NATHAN: Hell, they're all disgruntled! I ain't runnin' a damn daisy farm!

COP: What did the pyjamas—

NATHAN: My motto is do it my way or watch your butt!

COP: What did the pyjamas—

FBI 1:   So you think it might have been an employee?

NATHAN: Don't make me laugh. Without my say-so they don't piss with their pants on fire.

COP: What did the pyjamas look like?

FBI 1 (*pained*):   Officer—

NATHAN (*bellowing*):   I dunno, they were jammies! They had Yodas'n shit on 'em!

BELLOWING VOICE OFFSCREEN: Would ya mind, I'm trying to set up a Command Post here!

   NATHAN bellows back:

NATHAN: Get your feet off m'damn coffee table!

   Also raising his voice at the offscreen bellower:

FBI 1:   Ron, you're upsetting the victim.

   NATHAN is getting worked up.

NATHAN: Damnit, are you boys gonna go chase down your leads or are you gonna sit drinkin' coffee in the one house in the state where I know my boy ain't at?!

FBI 2:   Sir, there aren't any "leads" yet, aside from this coat—

NATHAN: Gimme that!

He grabs the overcoat being displayed by FBI 2.

NATHAN: That's a five-hundred-dollar camel's hair—

BYRUM: Sir, you might want to wash your hands at this point.

NATHAN realizes that he's gotten ink from his fingerprinting all over the coat.

NATHAN: Well goddamnit!

He is rising to his feet and hurling the coat to the floor.

. . . No leads?!

He furiously kicks the coat.

. . . Everyone leaves microbes'n whatnot!

Throughout the speech NATHAN stalks the room, working himself into a frenzy, furiously putting coffee cups onto coasters, generally cleaning up, hectoring the police, and swiping their feet off his furniture.

. . . Hell, that's your forte, trackin' down them microbes left by criminals'n commies'n shit! That's yer whole damn raison d'être! No leads?! I want Nathan Jr. back, or whichever the hell one they took! He's out there *some*where! Somethin' *leads* to him! And anyone can find him knows the difference between a lead and a hole in the ground!!

A HOLE IN THE GROUND   DAY

Specifically, it is the hole in the muddy patch of earth that GALE and EVELLE climbed out of. We hear only the squish-

suck of many feet walking around in the mud offscreen.

We are pulling back to reveal the feet—the shiny black
patent leather shoes and blue pants cuffs—becoming quickly
spattered—of several policemen milling about the hole.
German shepherds sniff around also.

With a roar, motorcycle wheels enter frame. The bike's
jackbooted rider casually tools around the hole once; police
step back and dogs skitter away to give him room.

He backs toward the camera and stops, standing astride the
bike. The burning stub of a cheroot is dropped into frame; it
hisses angrily and dies in the mud. We start to crane up.

The whipcracking BIKER cue mixes up. The BIKER's
motorcycle idles with a deep rumble, like the roar of fire on
the sun.

We are now framed looking over the BIKER's shoulder. The
policemen's attitude to him seems to be deferential. One cop
in front of him is pointing a direction. The BIKER is shaking
his head; he doesn't think they went that way.

Suddenly, with a loud whipcrack effect, the BIKER's head
snaps to profile. He is staring across the field, stock-still,
having heard, smelled or sensed something.

The dogs milling around the hole also react, snapping to
attention, a split second after the BIKER.

THEIR POV

A jackrabbit is bounding away at the far end of the field.

THE DOGS

After a moment, their attention returns to the hole.

THE BIKER

His attention also returns to the matter at hand. He squints,
concentrating. His bike rumbles. Gradually his face sets in a
specific direction.

We pan down to the tattoo on his shoulder: ''Mama Didn't
Love Me.'' His shoulder flexes once or twice as he revs the

*throttle; then he puts the bike in gear and it roars out of
frame.*

TRAILER KITCHEN   CLOSE ON GALE AND EVELLE

*They are both intently munching cornflakes, staring at
something offscreen. After a beat:*

EVELLE: . . . Awful good cereal flakes, Miz
McDunnough.

THEIR POV

ED *is sitting in the living room, bottle-feeding* NATHAN JR.
*She is surrounded by the rumpled sheets and blankets used by
the house guests. She does not respond to the ice-breaker.*

GALE *puts his spoon down and picks up a cigarette which
has been smoking in the ashtray next to him. There is a bead
of milk dribbling down his chin.*

He takes a contemplative puff, studying ED.

William Forsythe (Evelle) and John Goodman (Gale)

GALE: . . . Whyncha breast feed him? You 'pear to be capable.

ED: Mind your own bidnis.

Through a mouthful of cornflakes:

EVELLE: Ya don't breast feed him, he'll hate you for it later. That's why we wound up in prison.

GALE blows out smoke and picks up his spoon to start back in on his cornflakes.

GALE: Anyway, that's what Doc Schwartz tells us.

HI is walking in, yawning.

HI: Boys.

EVELLE: Mornin', H.I.

Sharply, as HI sits and starts to pour cornflakes into a bowl:

ED: . . . Hi.

HI holds the cornflakes box arrested in mid-air. He looks at ED, who is motioning to GALE and EVELLE with her eyes.

HI: Oh yeah . . . Say boys, you wouldn't mind makin' yourself scarce for a couple hours this afternoon?

ED: We're havin' some *decent* friends over.

GALE and EVELLE are looking dumbly from ED to HI.

HI: Heh-heh . . . What Ed means to say is, seein' as you two boys are wanted, it wouldn't exactly do to have folks seein' you here—I mean for your own protection.

GALE: Sure H.I.

EVELLE: Anything you say.

More relaxed now, to ED:

HI: Matter of fact honey, maybe I'll skip this little get-together myself, Glen won't mind, and I'll just duck out with the boys, knock back a couple of—uh, Co'Colas—

GALE: Sure H.I.

EVELLE: We'd love to have ya.

CLOSE ON ED

Looking pleadingly at HI.

BACK TO HI

Feeling the look, he goes back to his cornflakes.

HI: . . . Well . . . maybe that ain't such a hot idea either.

GALE *leans back to blow smoke at the ceiling.*

GALE (*bitterly*):   So many social engagements. So little time.

WIDE SHOT   GAS STATION BATHROOM

It is the bathroom where we earlier saw GALE *and* EVELLE *combing their hair, now empty.*
    We are looking toward the door. The bathroom is quiet except for the dripping sink, and the faint rumble of an approaching motorcycle. It grows louder, then begins to recede as the bike shoots by the station.
    Suddenly we hear the screech of the bike's brakes.

EXT THE STATION

We are on the road outside the gas station as the motorcycle screeches to a halt in the foreground. The low wide shot crops the BIKER at his shins. In the background behind him is the gas station.

The BIKER pauses for a moment, thinking or feeling.

BACK TO INT BATHROOM

We hear the rumble of the bike approaching, very loud.

CRASH—the bathroom door flies open as the BIKER bursts in astride his hog, bright daylight streaming in with him to throw him into imposing silhouette. The shafts of light pouring in are defined by motes of dust dancing in the air.

HIS POV

Fast track in on the jar of hair jelly sitting on the shelf under the mirror.

BACK TO BIKER

An extreme close shot shows his nostrils dilating as we hear him sniff.

He revs the rumbling bike, stealing thunder from a far mountain.

FRONT STOOP OF TRAILER

HI, with ED standing by, is just opening the door to a young couple. GLEN is a short stocky blond man in his early thirties, wearing Bermuda shorts. DOT is wearing slacks, heels, and a scarf over her hair.

HI: Glen, Dot—

As the door opens, DOT hops up the stoop shrieking.

DOT: Where's at baby? Where's he at?

From behind, GLEN *gives her an energetic THWOK on the ass.*

GLEN: Go find him honey!

DOT *spins and smacks* GLEN *across the face with her purse.
Through clenched teeth:*

DOT: Cut it out, Glen!

He reels under the blow.

ED (*quietly*):   He's asleep right now.

DOT *shrieks again, but this time muffles it with her own
hand. She tiptoes into the trailer, hand to her mouth.*
    GLEN, *rubbing his cheek, seems angry at himself.*

GLEN: Shit, I hope we didn't wake it!

DOT: Can I just sneak a peek-a-loo?

GLEN, *at the top of the stoop, turns out to the yard.*

GLEN: Come on kids . . .

WIDE SHOT   GLEN AND DOT'S KIDS

*A scad of children, ranging in age from two to seven, are
crawling over* HI's *car. One is beating on it with a large stick,
another sits on the hood pulling back one of the windshield
wipers, etc.*

GLEN: . . . Get away from Mr. McDunnough's car.

TRAILER BEDROOM

As ED *and* DOT *enter,* ED *beaming as they go to the crib.*

DOT: What's his name?

ED: Uh . . . Hi Jr. Till we think of a better one.

DOT: Whyncha call him Jason? I love Biblical names. If I had another little boy I'd name him Jason or Caleb or Tab. Oh!—

She puts her hand to her forehead, reacting to the baby as if she is about to faint.

. . . He's an angel!

She hides her face in her hands and looks away as if blinded, then sneaks a look around her hands.

Frances McDormand (Dot) and Holly Hunter

. . . He's an angel straight from heaven! Now honey I had all my kids the hard way so you gotta tell me where you got this angel. Did he fly straight down from heaven?

ED: Well—

DOT: You gonna send him to Arizona State?

TRAILER LIVING ROOM/KITCHEN

The weaving knee-level tracking shot is following a six-year-old boy in shorts and a dirty T-shirt as he tramps around the trailer, brandishing a big stick. He strikes the walls, furniture, various other objects with his stick, hollering "Bam! Bam-Bam!" with each blow.

The track weaves off him and onto HI, who is bending down to pull a couple of beers from the refrigerator. He raises his voice to make himself heard over the din of all the children boiling around the room:

HI: Need a beer, Glen?

GLEN: Does the Pope wear a funny hat?

HI considers this.

HI: . . . Well yeah, Glen, I guess it is kinda funny.

GLEN: Say, that reminds me! How many Pollacks it take to screw up a lightbulb?

HI: I don't know Glen, one?

HI looks down.
One of GLEN's children, in a cowboy hat, is squirting a squirt gun into his crotch area.

GLEN: Nope, it takes three!

He starts laughing, then catches himself.

. . . Wait a minute, I told it wrong. Here, I'm startin'
over: How come it takes three Pollacks to screw up a
lightbulb?

HI: I don't know, Glen.

GLEN: Cause they're so durn stupid!

He laughs; HI *doesn't react.*

. . . Shit man, loosen up! Don't ya get it?

HI *looks over at the TV, which the bam-shouting six-year-old
is banging with his stick.*

HI: No Glen, I sure don't.

GLEN: Shit man, think about it! I guess it's what they
call a Way Homer.

HI: Why's that?

GLEN: Cause you only get it on the Way Home.

HI: I'm already home, Glen.

The kid in the cowboy hat is reaching up to slap HI *on the ass.*

KID: You wetchaseff! Mr. McDunnough wet hisseff,
Daddy!

GLEN: Say, that reminds me! How'd you get that kid s'darned fast? Me'n Dottie went in to adopt on account of something went wrong with m'semen, and they told us five years' wait for a healthy white baby! I said healthy white baby! Five years! Okay, what else you got? Said, two Koreans and one Negro born with the heart outside . . .

He takes a sip of beer.

. . . Yeah, it's a crazy world.

HI: Someone oughta sell tickets.

GLEN: Sure, I'd buy one.

*HI is looking at another child who is just finishing off the T in
FART in crayon on the wall.
    GLEN chuckles, looking at his errant child.*

. . . That Buford's a sly one. Already knows his ABCs. But I'm sayin', how'd ya get the kid?

HI: Well this whole thing is just who knows who and favoritism. Ed has a friend at one of the agencies.

GLEN: Well maybe she can do something for me'n Dot. See there's something wrong with m'semen. Say, that reminds me! What you gonna call him?

HI: Uh, Ed—Ed Jr.

GLEN: Thought you said he was a boy.

HI: Well, as in Edward. Just like that name.

GLEN (*not really interested*):   Yeah, it's a good one . . .
Course I don't really need another kid, but Dottie says
these-here are gettin' too big to cuddle. Say, that reminds
me!—

There is the sound of shattering glass. GLEN *looks around.*

GLEN: Mind ya don't cutchaseff, Mordecai . . .

EXT PICNIC GROUNDS

DOT *faces* HI *and* ED *across a picnic table covered with grilled
hamburgers, rolls, green jello mold, cooler, etc.*
   *One of the younger children sits in the middle of the table,
occasionally taking a fistful of jello and flinging it at* HI. *The
two women don't seem to notice.*

DOT: —and then there's diphtheria-tetanus, what they
call dip-tet. You gotta get him dip-tet boosters yearly or
else he'll get lockjaw and night vision. Then there's the
smallpox vaccine, chicken pox and measles, and if your
kid's like ours you gotta take all those shots first to get
him to take 'em. Who's your pediatrician, anyway?

ED: We ain't exactly fixed on one yet. Have we Hi?

HI *sits stock-still with a stony face.*

. . . No, I guess we don't have one yet.

DOT *shrieks.*

DOT: Well you just gotta have one! You just gotta have
one this instant!

ED: Yeah, what if the baby gets sick, honey?

DOT: Hell, even if he don't get sick he's gotta have his dip-tet!

ED: He's gotta have his dip-tet, honey.

HI shrugs, then flinches as a piece of jello hits his shoulder.

HI: . . . Uh-huh.

DOT: You started his bank accounts?

ED: Have we done that honey? We gotta do that honey. What's that for, Dot?

DOT: That-there's for his orthodonture and his college. You soak his thumb in iodine you might get by without the orthodonture, but it won't knock any off the college.

HI sits stoically. DOT is looking offscreen:

. . . Reilly, take that diaper off your head and put it back on your sister! . . . Anyway, you probably got the life insurance all squared away.

ED: You done that yet honey?

DOT: You gotta do that, Hi! Ed here's got her hands full with that little angel!

HI (*dully*): Yes ma'am.

DOT: What would Ed and the angel do if a truck came along and splattered your brains all over the interstate? Where would you be then?

ED: Yeah honey, what if you get run over?

DOT: Or you got carried off by a twister?

LAKESIDE PATH

We are tracking on HI *and* GLEN *as they walk side by side.*
GLEN *is sopping wet, wearing only swimming suit and wing-
tipped shoes. His body is ghostly pale except for a V-area at
his neck and his arms below the short-sleeve line, which are a
bright angry red.*

GLEN: Hear about the person of the Polish persuasion
he walks into a bar holdin' a pile of shit in his hands,
says "Look what I almost stepped in."

GLEN bursts out laughing; HI *walks on in silence.*

HI: . . . Yeah, that's funny all right . . .

GLEN: Ya damn right it's funny! Shit man, what's the
matter?

HI: I dunno . . . maybe it's wife, kids, family life . . . I
mean are you, uh, satisfied Glen? Don't y'ever feel
suffocated? Like, like there's somethin' big pressin'
down . . .

GLEN (*solemnly*):   Eeeeeyep . . . I *do* know the feelin'.

HI shakes his head.

HI: I dunno—

GLEN: And I *told* Dottie to lose some weight but she
don't wanna listen!

He roars with laughter and slaps HI *heartily on the back. As
he chuckles sympathetically:*

. . . No man, I know what you mean. You got all kinds a responsibilities now. You're married, ya got a kid, looks like your whole life's set down and where's the excitement?

HI: Yeah Glen, I guess that's it.

GLEN: Okay! That's the disease, but there is a cure.

HI: Yeah?

GLEN: Sure; Doctor Glen is tellin' ya you can heal thyself.

HI: What do I gotta do?

GLEN: Well you just gotta broaden your mind a little bit. I mean say I asked you, what do you think about Dot?

HI (*puzzled*):   Fine woman you got there.

GLEN is eyeing him shrewdly.

GLEN: Okay. Now it might not look like it, but lemme tell you something: She's a hellcat.

HI: That right?

GLEN: T-I-G-E-R.

HI: But what's that got to do with—

GLEN: Don't rush me!

He stops walking. HI stops also, looking at GLEN, still puzzled. GLEN lays a companionable hand on his shoulder.

. . . Now the thing about Dot is, she thinks—and she's told me this—

He looks around as if to make sure they are not being overheard. His tone is confidential.

. . . she thinks . . . you're cute.

HI looks suspiciously at GLEN's hand on his shoulder.

HI:　. . . Yeah. . . ?

GLEN nods energetically:

GLEN:　I'm crappin' you negative! And *I* could say the same about Ed!

Through tightly clenched teeth:

HI:　What're you talkin' about, Glen?

GLEN:　What'm I talkin' about?! I'm talkin' about sex, boy! What the hell're *you* talkin' about?! You know, "l'amour"?! I'm talkin' me'n Dot are Swingers! As in "to Swing"! Wife-swappin'! What they call nowadays Open Marriage!

Beaming, he takes his hand off HI's shoulder and spreads his arms.

GLEN:　I'm talkin' about the Sex Revolution! I'm talkin' about—

THWAK—HI's fist swings into frame to connect solidly with GLEN's jaw.
　GLEN's feet leave the ground. He flies back and lands in a heap.

LOW-ANGLE REVERSE

GLEN *in the foreground, groggily rubbing his jaw;* HI *approaching menacingly.*

HI: Keep your goddamned hands off my wife!

GLEN: Shit man!

He is scrambling to his feet.

. . . I was only tryin' to help!

HI: Keep your goddamned hands off my wife!

With HI *still advancing,* GLEN *starts to run.*

TRACKING ON GLEN

With HI *pursuing in the background.*
   GLEN *is looking back over his shoulder to shout at* HI *as he runs.*

GLEN: You're crazy! I feel pity for you, man! You—

*CRASH!—*GLEN *runs smack into a tree and drops like a sack of cement.*

INT CAR NIGHT

HI *is driving, his jaw rigidly set, his temple throbbing.*
NATHAN JR. *sits in a safety seat between him and* ED.

ED: We finally go out with some decent people and you break his nose. That ain't too funny, Hi.

HI (*stolidly*):   His kids seemed to think it was funny.

ED: Well they're just kids, you're a grown man with responsibilities. Whatever possessed you?

HI: He was provokin' me when I popped him.

ED: How'd he do that?

HI: . . . Never mind.

ED: But Hi, he's your foreman, he's just gonna fire you now.

HI: I expect he will.

ED: And where does that leave me and Nathan Jr.?

HI: With a man for a husband.

He is pulling into a convenience store parking lot.

ED: That ain't no answer.

HI: Honey, that's the only answer.

He puts the car in park but leaves it running.

. . . Nathan needs some Huggies. I'll be out directly.

As he gets out of the car:

. . . Mind you stay strapped in.

INT   STORE
CLOSE SHOT   L'EGGS RACK

A hand enters to take a package of panty hose from the standing rack.

CLOSE SHOT   HUGGIES

A hand enters to take a big carton of disposable diapers from the shelf.

CLOSE UP   CASHIER

A pimply-faced lad with a paper 7-Eleven cap on his head. He is looking up from a dirty magazine, reacting in horror to something approaching.

HIS POV

HI is approaching the check-out island with a gun in one hand, the carton of Huggies tucked under the other. The L'Eggs stocking is pulled over his head to distort his features.

HI: I'll be taking these Huggies and whatever cash you got.

CLOSE SHOT   CASHIER'S HAND

As he presses a silent alarm under the lip of his counter.

EXT   CAR

ED is reading to NATHAN JR. from a large picture book.

ED: "'Not by the hair of my chinny-chin-chin.' 'Then I'll huff and I'll puff . . .'"

She pauses for a moment, listening. We can barely hear a distant siren. She resumes absently, but her voice trails off:

"'. . . and I'll blow your house in . . .'"

We can definitely hear the WHOO-WHOO of the siren now, and it is definitely approaching. ED hooks an arm around the seat and looks behind the car, then looks forward.

HER POV

Indistinctly visible through the semi-reflective glass are two figures at the check-out island. One is pointing something at the other.

BACK TO ED

As the siren is growing louder. Under her breath:

ED: That son of a bitch.

She unstraps herself and gets out of the car.

INT   STORE

Two-shot of HI and the CASHIER, who is stuffing bills into a grocery bag. Beyond them we can see ED, outside, circling the front of the car.
   Her shout is muffled through the glass:

ED: You son of a bitch!

With this HI notices her. He turns to the CASHIER.

HI: Better hurry it up. I'm in dutch with the wife.

But ED is already getting into the driver's seat of the car.

BACK TO ED

As she slams the car door shut. The siren is quite loud now.

ED: That son of a bitch. Hang on, pumpkin.

The car squeals out of the lot.

WIDE SHOT   THE STREET

The squad car tops a rise to bounce into view, its siren wailing.

BACK TO THE STORE

HI *bursts out the door, still wearing the stocking. The carton of Huggies is still tucked under one arm.*

Bellowing hopefully after his departing car:

HI: Honey!

We hear the SMACK-CRACK of a gunshot and glass impact, but the approaching squad car is still too far down the block to have been the source.

HI *looks around the parking lot, bewildered.*

The wailing siren is becoming painfully loud.

HI *looks behind him at the plate-glass front of the store, where a bullet pock mars the glass.*

HIS POV

Through the glass we see the pimply young CASHIER with the paper 7-Eleven cap pop up from behind the counter to sight down his huge .44 Magnum for another shot. The gun is so big he uses both hands to heft it.

SMACK-CRACK—the bullet kisses another hole in the glass.

HI *is off and running.*

The squad car is screeching into the lot. An officer tumbles out of the passenger side before the car is fully stopped. He rolls on the pavement, then hurriedly rights himself and takes up a half-kneeling shooting stance.

At the same time the little CASHIER is emerging from the 7-Eleven with his gun.

The two bang away at HI's retreating figure—the POLICEMAN's revolver popping, the CASHIER's Magnum booming.

We hear the POLICEMAN who is still in the car drawling over its loudspeaker:

SPEAKER: Halt. It's a police warning, son. Put those groceries down and turn yourself in.

TRACKING ON HI

Legs pumping, panty hose still over his head, its unused leg streaming behind him like an aviator's scarf. The gun is tucked into his belt; the Huggies are tucked securely under his arm.

Behind him we can see the OFFICER *and the* CASHIER *squeeze off another couple shots, and then the policeman piles back into the squad car.*

ED'S CAR

Driving. She hears distant gunshots.

ED: That son of a bitch . . . Hold on, Nathan. We're gonna go pick up Daddy.

She hangs a vicious U-turn.

TRACKING ON HI

Huffing and puffing down the road with his Huggies.

The cop car careens onto the street in the background, its siren wailing.

The PASSENGER COP *is leaning far out his window, one hand gripping the light-and-siren rack, the other pointing a gun at* HI, *shooting away.*

Bullets whizz past.

Suddenly, with a soft pthunk! the Huggies box pops forward, out from under HI's *arm —hit by a bullet. Still running,* HI *reaches forward, tries to catch it on the fly, bobbles it, tips it—loses it. He overruns it a couple steps before he can bring himself up short.*

He turns and reaches to pick up the box but—PING-PING—bullets chew up the road near his hand.

Leaving the Huggies, HI *takes off through a well-manicured yard.*

The police car is proceeding on down the street to catch him around the corner, the driver still drawling over his loudspeaker:

SPEAKER: That's private property, son. Come back out to the street and reveal yourself to Officer Steensma and Officer Scott—that's me.

YARD

HI *vaults a fence to land in the backyard.*

As he straightens to his feet we hear a horrible snarling and barking.

A huge black Doberman is bounding across the lawn. It looks like it means to rip HI's *throat out.*

LOW TRACKING SHOT   TOWARD HI

The dog's racing POV as it bounds toward the paralyzed HI.

The dog leaps—camera flying up toward HI's *face—and:*

CLOSE SHOT   HI'S FROZEN PROFILE

The dog's slavering muzzle flies into frame and—stops, bare inches from HI's *nose, and the dog falls back, having reached the end of his chain.*

HI *resumes running.*

CLOSE

On the dog, snarling and straining against the end of his chain.

TRACKING

Down along the chain toward the spike mooring it to the ground. As the dog strains, the spike starts to stir in the ground.

Other dogs can be heard barking now, the Doberman having started a sympathetic wave.

ED'S CAR

Her jaw set, she takes a hard turn, looking this way and that.

ED: That son of a bitch . . .

The police car approaches and roars by, the PASSENGER COP *still hanging out his window.*

     . . . Lookie Nathan, a police car . . .

She is looking in her rearview mirror.

     . . . Say, that looks like Bill Steensma.

LOW TRACKING SHOT

The camera is shooting forward at ground level, following the Doberman as it bounds along. The Doberman is dragging his chain and spike, which stretch into the foreground, bumping and scraping along the road.
     Far ahead we can see HI *running, then turning down an intersecting street.*
     A second dog peels into the road to bound along with the Doberman.

TRACKING BEHIND HI

Running up a dark street. There is an oncoming pickup. HI *runs directly at it.*

INT PICKUP

The DRIVER *screams and brakes—not quite in time.*
     HI *rolls onto the hood, and off, and gamely trots over to open the passenger door.*
     The DRIVER *is leaning over to tell him:*

DRIVER: Son, you got a panty on your head.

HI: Just drive fast . . .

He is displaying his gun as he starts to climb in.

. . . and don't stop till I tell ya.

Before HI *can get his door shut the* DRIVER *is obediently peeling out.*
　　HI *is reacting to an oncoming car. He peels the stocking off to look, and leans across the* DRIVER'S *lap to bellow as* ED'S *car passes:*

HI:　　. . . Honey!

HI *turns to look through the back window.*

HIS POV

ED'S *car is braking and spinning into a U-turn.*

BACK TO HI

Leaning out the window.

HI:　　Mind the baby now!

Next to him, the DRIVER *is screaming.*
　　As HI *turns forward, the entire windshield explodes in.*

THEIR POV

The pimply-faced CASHIER *from the 7-Eleven is standing in the middle of the road ahead, sighting down his .44 Magnum for another shot.*
　　We are rushing in.

THE DRIVER

Still screaming.

THE CASHIER

Ready to fire and—THUMP—he is bowled over by the arriving Doberman, still trailing chain and spike, and now accompanied by three other dogs, all braying at the top of their lungs.

Still screaming, the DRIVER *puts his body into a hard right turn to avoid the* CASHIER *and hellhounds.*

NEW STREET

Roaring up the new street, they are now directly in the path of the oncoming police car, its siren wailing, barreling straight at them.

Still screaming, the DRIVER *leans into another hard right. Wind is whistling in through where the windshield used to be.*

Two wheels hop curb as the car skids into the new street, fishtails, and roars away.

ED'S CAR

She hears dogs, siren, squealing brakes on an adjacent street.

ED: Hold on Nathan, we'll take a shortcut.

She gives the wheel a hard right turn.

But there is no cross street. The car hops the curb and roars up someone's nicely tended front yard, heading for the gap between this house and the one next door.

POLICE CAR

Recovered and turned around from its near collision with the SCREAMING DRIVER, *the squad car is now squealing onto the street the* SCREAMER *swerved on to—resuming pursuit.*

As the police car roars down the street, ED'S *car appears from between two houses behind it, bounces down the front yard to the street and follows the police.*

SCREAMER'S PICKUP

Raking two-shot of HI *and the* SCREAMER. HI *is looking back over his shoulder at the pursuing police.*

Desperately pleading:

SCREAMER: Can I stop now?

HI looks forward.

HIS POV
They are rushing toward an imposing colonial house planted at the end of the dead-end street.

BACK TO HI
HI: Maybe you better.

CLOSE SHOT   BRAKE PEDAL
Stepped on hard. The brakes scream.

EXT   CAR
As the car squeals to a halt HI is catapulted through where the windshield used to be, tumbling over the hood onto the front lawn.

He rolls to his feet and, as he runs up the lawn, calls back over his shoulder:

HI: Thank you.

INTO THE HOUSE
We are tracking behind HI as he runs up to the house and crashes through the screen door.

Still tracking behind him as he runs through the living room.

A middle-aged couple sits on the couch watching TV. They look up as HI rushes by.

HI plunges down a staircase. As he does so we hear: ka-chick ka-chock ka-chick ka-chock.

He emerges into a rec room where he and we rush past two kids playing ping-pong. He runs out the back door.

TRACKING WITH THE POLICEMAN

As he runs into the house.

As he runs through the living room we catch a glimpse of the middle-aged couple gaping at him.

OFFICER STEENSMA *plunges down the stairs.*

TRACKING ON HI

Outdoors now, running, crossing the street behind the house and entering the parking lot of a supermarket on the other side.

BACK TO THE HOUSE

As a pack of dogs thunders in. The lead Doberman with chain and spike has now picked up about a dozen neighborhood dogs.

The dogs thunder through the living room and down the stairs. As they hit the rec room the thunder of their feet turns into the clatter of nails on tile.

INT   SUPERMARKET

As HI *bursts in. Tracking on him as he runs down the broad front aisle, head whipping as he runs, looking up each perpendicular lane, searching for something.*

He turns up one of the last lanes, races along it and grabs a carton of Huggies, still on the flat run.

He emerges into the broad back aisle and runs along it, but at the first perpendicular lane he hits, we see OFFICER STEENSMA, *gun leveled, at the other end. He fires.*

HI *keeps running.*

The POLICEMAN *is running along the front aisle, keeping pace with* HI *running along the back aisle. He squeezes off shots at* HI *as each lane gives him the opportunity.*

HI *abruptly stops between lanes and doubles back, losing the* POLICEMAN. *He runs down the second lane he comes to toward the front of the store.*

Cameraman Barry Sonnenfeld with Joel Coen and Ethan Coen

*The pack of dogs appears at the end of the lane and
thunders up toward* HI, *braying at the top of their doggy
lungs. The lead Doberman holds in his teeth a paper 7-Eleven
cap.*

HI *reverses again, and emerges into the back aisle.*

*BANG! A pyramid of cranberry juice explodes at his
shoulder. The* POLICEMAN *has been waiting at the end of the
back aisle; he aims once again.*

HI *plunges down the next lane but is brought up short as
KA-BOOM! five jars of applesauce explode in front of him.*
HI *looks.*

*Standing in the raised platform-cubicle at the front of the
store is the* STORE MANAGER, *a fat man in a white short-
sleeved shirt with a lit cigarette dangling from his mouth.*

The MANAGER *cracks open his shotgun and inserts two
more cartridges—thoonk thoonk—in the smoking chamber.*

HI *doubles back once again toward the back aisle.*

He is still several paces from the end of the lane when the
POLICEMAN *appears there, squaring to face him.*

The POLICEMAN *is in front of him. The* MANAGER *is blowing out groceries on the shelves behind him.*

CLOSE ON POLICEMAN

As he coolly levels his police special and takes aim at HI.

POLICEMAN'S POV

Still on the dead run, HI *is flinging the carton of Huggies. The carton rockets straight at the camera.*

BACK TO POLICEMAN

Futilely raising his gun to avoid—impact: The Huggies catch him square on the chest. The force makes him stumble one fatal step backwards—into the back aisle—where:

CRASH—He is hit broadside and bowled over by a rocketing shopping cart, propelled by an hysterically screaming SHOPPER.

TRACKING ON SHOPPER

Racing on down the back aisle, bellowing.

HER FEET

Tracking from in front. Beyond her we can see the pack of furiously barking dogs, nipping at her heels. They boil over the prostrate OFFICER STEENSMA, *and this is the last we see of him in this movie.*

EXT STORE

As HI *emerges through the back door.* ED *is just skidding around the corner.*

HI *scrambles in the passenger side.*

INT CAR

Raking two-shot with HI *in the foreground. The car peels out of the lot.*

HI: Thank you honey, you really didn't have to do this—

*THWAK—*ED *gives him a good hard slap and* HI*'s head rolls toward the camera.*

ED: You son of a bitch! You're actin' like a mad dog!

Rubbing his jaw:

HI: Turn left, honey.

Still at top speed, she leans into a hard left, tires squealing.

ED: What if me'n the baby'd been picked up? Nathan Jr. would a been accessory to armed robbery!

HI: Nawww honey, it ain't armed robbery if the gun ain't loaded—

ED: What kind of home life is this for a toddler?! You're supposed to be an example!

HI: Now honey, I never postured myself as the three-piece suit type—Turn left, dear.

ED: We got a child now, everything's changed!

HI: Well Nathan Jr. accepts me for what I am and I think you better had, too. You know, honey, I'm okay you're okay? That-there's what it is.

ED: I know, but honey—

HI: See I come from a long line of frontiersmen and— here it is, turn here dear—frontiersmen and outdoor types.

HI's eyes are fixed on something in the road ahead.

ED: I'm not gonna live this way, Hi. It just ain't family life!

HI's attention is still on the road. He is opening his door, even though the car is still racing along. He absently concedes:

HI: Well . . . It ain't Ozzie and Harriet.

LOW ANGLE   THE STREET

In the extreme foreground sits the first carton of Huggies that HI dropped in the middle of the road. The car is approaching.
   As the car passes the carton, HI's hand reaches from the passenger door and snags it.

REVERSE

As HI pulls the carton in and slams his door shut. Crane up on the car speeding away.

TRAILER LIVING ROOM

As ED bursts in the front door, holding NATHAN JR.

ED: You two are leaving.

ON GALE AND EVELLE

They look up, dumbstruck and mortified, from the sofa where they have been watching TV.

ED: Tomorrow morning. Now I got nothing against you personally . . .

GALE and EVELLE look appealingly toward HI, who shifts uncomfortably behind ED.

ED: . . . but you're wanted by the authorities and you're a bad influence in this household, in my opinion.

GALE: Well ma'am . . . we sure didn't mean to influence anyone.

EVELLE: And if we did, we apologize.

ED is unmoved.

ED: I'm goin' in to town tomorrow to see about some shots for the baby. When I come back you better be gone or I'll kick you out myself.

She storms into the bedroom and slams the door.
There is an awkward silence as GALE studies his thumb and EVELLE stares at the ceiling. Finally EVELLE turns to HI.

EVELLE: . . . What's he need, his dip-tet?

HI: I'm awful sorry boys, but when Ed gets mad, you know, when she gets an idea . . .

GALE: Well there ain't a thing to apologize for, H.I. . . .

He looks at EVELLE.

. . . It seems pretty clear what the situation is here.

EVELLE: Yeah, I guess the Missus wants us to clear out.

GALE: Now H.I., you'll pardon me for sayin' so, but I get the feelin' that this-here . . .

His gesture seems to take in the trailer and the entire domestic situation.

. . . ain't exactly workin' out.

HI: Well now Ed's generally a real sweetheart, I—

GALE: And as per usual, I wouldn't be surprised if the source of the marital friction was financial.

HI: Well, matter of fact, I did lose my job today—

EVELLE: Come on Hi, you're young, you got your health—what do you want with a job?

GALE: But look, I'd rather light a candle than curse your darkness. As you know, Evelle'n I never go anywhere without a reason . . . and here we are in your little domicile. We come to invite you in on a score.

EVELLE: A bank, Hi.

HI is shaking his head.

HI: Aw boys, I don't—

GALE: I know you're partial to convenience stores but, H.I., the sun don't rise and set on the corner grocery.

EVELLE: It's like Doc Schwartz says: You gotta have a little ambition. Why we just heard on the news how somebody snatched off one of the Arizona babies. Now there's someone thinkin' big.

GALE: And here you are sittin' around on your butt playin' house with a—don't get me wrong, H.I., with a fine woman—but a woman who needs the button-down type.

HI: Well now that ain't really any of your—

GALE: Just lookahere . . .

He is handing HI *a folded-up picture.*

EVELLE: Picture of El Dorado, Hi.

GALE: Though the locals call it the Farmers and Mechanics Bank of LaGrange. Looks like a hayseed bank and, tell you the truth, it *is* a hayseed bank. Except the last Friday of every financial quarter there's more cash in that bank than flies at a barbecue.

EVELLE: And guess what day it is tomorrow?

GALE: Ya see, H.I., it's when the hayseeds come in to cash their farm subsidy checks.

EVELLE: A-One information.

GALE: Got it in the joint from a guy named Lawrence Spivey, one of Dick Nixon's undersecretaries of agriculture.

EVELLE: He's in for solicitin' sex from a state trooper.

GALE: Ordinarily we don't associate with that class of person, but . . .

GALE chuckles.

. . . he was tryin' to make brownie points with some of the boys.

HI: Boys, I can't—

EVELLE: We need someone handy with a scatter-gun to cover the hayseeds while we get the cash.

GALE: Y'understand, H.I., if this works out it's just the beginning of a spree across the entire Southwest proper. We keep goin' till we can retire—or we get caught.

EVELLE: Either way we're fixed for life.

HI is still shaking his head.

HI: Boys, it's a kind offer, but you're suggesting I just up'n leave Ed. Now that'd be pretty damn cowardly, wouldn't it.

GALE: Would it? Think about it, H.I. Seems to me, stayin' here, y'ain't doin' her any good. And y'ain't bein' true to your own nature.

The camera has floated in to a close shot of HI, staring glumly at GALE.

TRACKING ON MOTORCYCLE   NIGHT

Following it, very close, we see only its rear wheel and fender and twin exhaust pipes, one on either side. Flame is boiling in each exhaust pipe as the hog roars.

HIGHER TRACKING SHOT

From behind the BIKER's head as he rides through the night. With the sharp whipcrack effect he suddenly looks left, searching. With a second whipcrack effect he suddenly looks right, still searching.
    He banks into a turn.

EXT   TRAILER

Creeping in. Late at night. We are tracking in toward the one window that is illuminated, with a feeble yellow light.
   In voice-over, HI *is composing a letter.*

VO: My dearest Edwinna. Tonight as you and Nathan slumber, my heart is filled with anguish . . .

DISSOLVE THROUGH TO:
INT   TRAILER

Creeping in on HI*'s hunched back, as he sits over the kitchen table writing the letter. The yellow lamp sitting on the table is the only light on in the trailer.*

VO: . . . I hope that you will both understand, and forgive me for what I have decided I must do. By the time you read this, I will be gone.

DISSOLVE THROUGH TO:
LIVING ROOM

Creeping in on GALE *and* EVELLE, *sprawled on the sofa and easy chair respectively, sawing boards.*

VO: . . . I will never be the man that you want me to be, the husband and father that you and Nathan deserve . . .

DISSOLVE THROUGH:
BACK TO HI

Still creeping in.

VO: Maybe it's my upbringing; maybe it's just that my genes got screwed up—I don't know . . .

DISSOLVE THROUGH TO:
INT 7-ELEVEN

Creeping in on the pimply-faced CASHIER, *sitting asleep behind the counter, a dirty magazine lying face-down, open on his chest.*

VO: But the events of the last day have showed, amply, that I don't have the strength of character to raise up a family . . .

We are slowly panning over to the newspaper rack, revealing tomorrow's headline: WHERE IS NATHAN JR.?

. . . in the manner befitting a responsible adult, and not like the wild man from Borneo.

DISSOLVE THROUGH TO:
ARIZONA HOME

Creeping in on NATHAN SR. *in the living room, asleep in his ottoman armchair, lit only by the snow from the TV set he is facing, a half-full glass of milk on the coffee table next to him.*
  His robe is disheveled; his eyeglasses have slid down his nose.

VO: . . . I say all this to my shame.

DISSOLVE THROUGH TO:
TRAILER BEDROOM

Creeping in on ED *and* NATHAN JR., *asleep together in the double bed.* ED's *arm is draped protectively over the sleeping infant.*

VO: . . . I will love you always, truly and deeply. But I fear that if I stay I would only bring bad trouble . . .

We start to hear the rumble of the motorcycle mix up again.

. . . on the heads of you and Nathan Jr.

DISSOLVE THROUGH TO:
BLACKNESS

Night sky. The motorcycle tire enters frame as the bike comes to a halt. The BIKER *plants a jackbooted foot in the foreground.*
The engine rumbles.

VO: I feel the thunder gathering even now; if I leave, hopefully, it will leave with me.

We are craning up over the BIKER*'s back to reveal what he is looking at: We are on a bluff overlooking the trailer park. In the window of one trailer below, a yellow light glows.*

. . . I cannot tarry . . .

DISSOLVE THROUGH:
BACK TO HI

Still creeping in.

VO: Better I should go, send you money, and let you curse my name. Your loving . . . Herbert.

FADE OUT
FIRE

Roaring at the cut. Through it we can see the BIKER *sitting on the ground, legs stretched out in front of him, back resting against his parked motorcycle, arms folded across his chest.*
Perfectly motionless, he stares at the campfire.
We are floating in toward him.
As we come closer, eventually drawing in to a close shot of his face, we gradually realize something peculiar about his

eyes: He seems to have none. Although his eyes are unblinkingly open we do not see eyeballs, but only fire— either a reflection of the campfire or something roaring— burning—inside.

CLOSE SHOT   DOOR MAT

It reads: "Come On In! To Unpainted Arizona."
The smoking butt of a cheroot is dropped onto the mat. A jackbooted foot grinds it out.

CLOSE SHOT   BAR ON GLASS DOOR

Leading into the showroom. The BIKER's *mail-and-chained fist pushes the door open.*

LOW WIDE TRACKING SHOT

Behind the jackboots as they stroll through a showroom of unpainted furniture and bathroom fixtures.

TRACKING ON THE MAILED HAND

Swinging as he walks, the BIKER's *hand produces a fresh cheroot from no apparent source—either sleight-of-hand or magic.*

THE OTHER HAND

Similarly producing a long wooden match.

DISCOLORED TEETH

Biting down on the cigar.

HAND

Dragging the kitchen match along the unfinished wood surface of an expensive bureau, leaving an ugly black scar. The match erupts into roaring flame.

CIGAR

Crackling as it is lit.

DOOR

Reading "Executive Offices." The mailed fist pushes it open.

PEBBLED GLASS DOOR

From the inside of the office. The name on the pebbled glass is a backwards NATHAN ARIZONA.

There is the shadow of a man approaching the door, and muffled voices.

SECRETARY'S VOICE: I'm sorry, Mr. Arizona, he just barged in . . .

The door swings open and NATHAN stands looking in, his middle-aged secretary hanging at his elbow.

. . . Should I call Dewayne?

NATHAN is staring toward his desk.

NATHAN: Hell no, why wake the security guard. I'll take care a this.

The secretary leaves.

NATHAN'S POV

The BIKER sits with his back to us, jackboots propped lazily on the desk.

His head bobs and ducks, as if he is following some movement in the air in front of him.

BACK TO NATHAN

Eyes on the BIKER he slams the door shut behind him, looking for some reaction.

BIKER

No reaction. His head continues to bob and duck.

BACK TO NATHAN

Circling the BIKER *as he crosses to sit behind his desk.*

HIS POV

Arcing around to reveal the BIKER's *face. He still does not react to* NATHAN, *not even bothering to give him a glance. His eyes continue to follow some phantom movement.*

When the BIKER *speaks it is still without looking at* NATHAN, *and with a surprisingly soft voice and mild, unhurried manner:*

BIKER: You got flies.

He finally looks at NATHAN, *and smiles faintly.*

NATHAN: I doubt it. This place's climate-controlled, all the windows are sealed. Who the hell are you?

BIKER: Name of Leonard Smalls. My friends call me Lenny . . .

He takes a drag on his cigar.

. . . Only I ain't got no friends.

NATHAN: Stop, you'll make me bust out crying. Listen Leonard, you want some furniture or a shitbox, they're out on the sales floor.

SMALLS *is pleasantly shaking his head.*

SMALLS: Nooo, I ain't a customer, I'm a manhunter. Ordinarily. Though I do hunt babies, on occasion. Hear you got one you can't put your hand to.

NATHAN: What do you know about it?

SMALLS: Wal, that's my business. I'm a tracker—part
Hopi Indian, some say part hound dog. When some dink
skips bail, crushes outta the joint, I'm the man they call.

NATHAN: Mister, I got the cops, the state troopers and
the Federal-B-I already lookin' for my boy. Now if you
got information I *strongly* advise—

SMALLS: Cop won't find your boy. Cop couldn't find
his own butt if it had a bell on it. Wanna find an outlaw,
call an outlaw. Wanna find a Dunkin Donuts, call a cop.

NATHAN: Smalls, first off, take your damn feet off
m'furniture. Second off, it's widely known I posted a
twenty grand reward for my boy. If you can find him,
claim it. Short of that what do we got to talk about?

SMALLS: Price. Fair price. And that ain't whatever you
say it is; fair price is what the market'll bear. Now there
are people, mind you, there are people in this land,
who'll pay a lot more'n twenty grand for a healthy baby.

  NATHAN is looking at him stonily.

NATHAN: What're you after?

SMALLS: Give you an idea, when I was a lad I m'self
fetched twenty-*five* thousand on the black market. And
them's 1954 dollars. I'm sayin, fair price. For *fifty* grand
I'll track him, find him—

  *Quick as a flash the heretofore languid SMALLS bolts forward,
  his fist stopped an inch short of NATHAN's nose.*

EXTREME CLOSE SHOT   SMALLS' FINGERS

His index finger and thumb are pinched together—holding the leg of a struggling fly that he has just plucked from the air.

SMALLS: . . . and the people that took him . . .

He flicks the fly away.

. . . I'll kick their butts.

He sits back down.

. . . No extra charge.

NATHAN *stares grimly at* SMALLS.

NATHAN: And if I don't pay?

SMALLS: Oh I'll get your boy regardless. Cause if *you* don't pay, the market will.

NATHAN: You wanna know what I think? I think you're an evil man. I think this is nothin' but a goddamn screw job. I think it's a shakedown. I think you're the one took Nathan Jr. and my fine friend, I think you're the one gonna get his butt kicked . . .

NATHAN *swivels to punch numbers on a telephone.*

. . . I think I'm on the phone to the cops right now, and I—

He swivels back, looking up, and his speech stops short.

HIS POV

The office is empty. A whipcrack effect builds to the cut and:

CLOSE ON HI

His eyes snap open as the whipcrack echoes away.
He has been slumped over the kitchen table, asleep.

GALE (*os*):   Up and attem, H.I. Today is the first day of the rest of your life . . .

EVELLE (*os*):   . . . and already you're fuckin' it up.

HI looks up.
GALE and EVELLE are smiling down at him.

EVELLE: Come on, the missus'll be back from town soon.

HI takes the envelope that he was slumped over, TO ED written on its face. As he sticks it to the refrigerator door with a broccoli magnet:

HI: Where's the baby?

EVELLE: Bedroom, in his crib.

GALE: He's sawin' toothpicks, he'll be fine.

There is a harsh knock at the door. All three tense.

. . . You expectin' anybody?

HI is staring. The knock comes again.

HI: No. You two stay outta sight.

He goes to the door, pulls back its shade and peeks out. Under his breath:

HI: Shit.

He opens the door.

EXT TRAILER

It is GLEN. *He backs nervously down to the foot of the stoop as* HI *stands in the half-open doorway.* GLEN *comes to rest a few feet away from the stoop.*
    He is wearing a neckbrace. The bridge of his eyeglasses is taped together. Cotton wadding is stuffed up his nose, which is darkly discolored. He holds a rolled up newspaper.
    His station wagon is parked behind him, idling.

HI: Morning Glen.

GLEN *speaks in a very nasal voice:*

GLEN: I ain't comin' in if ya don't mind. I'll just keep my distance.

HI: I didn't invite you in, Glen.

GLEN: Well don't even bother. First off, you're fired—and that's official.

HI: I kinda figured that, Glen.

GLEN: Well that ain't why I'm here neither. No sir. You're in a whole shitload of trouble, my friend.

    HI *is looking at him evenly.*

HI: Why don't you just calm down, Glen.

GLEN: Why don't you make me?! Know that little baby you got in there? Remember him? I know what his real name is!

HI is suddenly nervous and urgent:

HI: Wanna keep your voice down, Glen?

GLEN: I'll pitch my voice wherever I please! His name ain't Hi Jr.! His name ain't Ed Jr.! But it's Junior all right! Yes sir, it's *Nathan* Jr.!

HI takes one step down holding out a calming hand.
GLEN takes two nervous steps away and reassures himself by resting a hand on the door of his station wagon.

. . . Stay away from me, McDunnough!

HI stops short. GLEN smiles.

GLEN: . . . Sure, you're an awful big man when you got somethin' around to clobber a guy with!

HI (*softly*):   I ain't a big man.

GLEN: That's right! And now you're at my mercy!

He spits on the dirt in front of him.

. . . I'm your worst nightmare! I wanted to just turn you in for the re-ward. But Dot, she wants something to cuddle. So it looks like that baby's gonna be *Glen* Jr. from now on!

HI's face is set in rigid dismay.

. . . I'll give you a day to break the news to Ed . . .

GLEN *is getting into his car.*

. . . Dot'll be by tomorrow to pick him up.

He slams the door.

. . . It's either that or jail. Oh and say, that reminds me! You'll find a doctor bill in the mail in a few days. I recommend you pay it!

And the car squeals off.
HI looks back at the trailer.

HIS POV

A slat in the window blind drops back into place.

BACK TO HI

He opens the door.

INT   TRAILER

EVELLE *is already emerging from the bedroom with the baby in his arms.*
HI moves toward EVELLE. *His teeth are set; he means business.*

HI: What's goin' on here.

GALE *steps in front of* HI.

GALE: You know what's goin' on, H.I. It's just business. Now this can go either hard or easy—

HI gives GALE *a hard push to get past him.* GALE *staggers back but recovers and grabs* HI *in a bear hug.*
HI flips GALE. GALE *lands on a coffee table which flips up and crashes back down.*

EVELLE is dancing back out of HI's reach. As HI lunges for him the prostrate GALE grabs his legs.

HI goes down hard.

GALE leaps to his feet and—CRASH—bangs his head up against an overhanging lamp. Both of his hands fly up to massage the top of his head.

THOOMP—HI's fist flies into frame to connect with GALE's unguarded stomach. GALE doubles over, clutching at his gut.

HI interlaces his fingers to make a club of his two hands. With GALE's bowed head a target in front of him, HI swings his hands up over his head.

HI's knuckles scrape painfully against the plaster of the too-low ceiling. Skin is flayed, plaster crumbles.

HI grabs at his knuckles in pain. GALE lunges with a mid-body tackle that sends HI crashing into the wall.

GALE, still on top of him, reaches back to throw a punch. The reach-back sends his elbow crashing through a window but doesn't stop the punch.

It connects with HI's jaw.

GALE throws another quick punch, all his weight behind it. HI's head bobs sideways just in time and GALE's fist goes through the wall. It is momentarily stuck there.

HI uses the opportunity to grab GALE's one free arm with both of his. He is twisting it to make GALE, roaring with pain, twist around and present his back to him.

HI climbs aboard, grabbing GALE's face.

GALE, still roaring, is pulling his fist out of the hole. He grabs a lath exposed by the hole and pulls; it tears out of the wall and snaps free, giving him a length of about two feet.

GALE is rampaging around like a grizzly bear hemmed in a too-small space. HI is hanging on for dear life, his own feet flailing this way and that, knocking over lamps and wall fixtures as GALE bends and twirls about, trying to shake him loose. GALE crashes and bounces off the walls, roaring in pain and fury.

Close shots of GALE'S *face show his features impossibly and grotesquely contorted by* HI'S *hand, squeezing, gripping and clutching at it.*

EVELLE *is dancing around with the baby, dodging crashing furniture and flailing body parts.*

EXT WIDE SHOT THE TRAILER

At the cut GALE'S *roaring drops out. We hear the chirping of birds and the laughter of children playing in the neighborhood.*

It is a sunny day.

BACK TO INT TRAILER

GALE *still roars. With a last mighty effort, he finally swings* HI *off his body.*

HI *crashes against a wall and through it to land in the:*

BATHROOM

Amid a shower of plaster dust and lath. HI *has landed, groggily, against the toilet.*

EVELLE *enters now with his hands free, apparently having set the baby down somewhere.*

He yanks the cord off the bathroom blinds.

LIVING ROOM

HI *is seated in a straight-back chair, still violently struggling but* GALE'S *arms are wrapped around him from behind.*

EVELLE *is just finishing tying off his wrists behind the chair.*

No one talks; there is nothing left to say.

Finished, GALE *goes to the door and* EVELLE *goes to the bedroom. He emerges with the baby and precedes* GALE *out the door,* GALE *slamming it behind him.*

HI *starts bucking and struggling, weeping tears of rage and frustration. He succeeds only in tipping forward, face down into the carpet, the strapped-on chair pressing down on top of him.*

His profile is pressed into the carpet.

Offscreen we hear the door of the trailer opening.

HI'S POV

At carpet level. GALE's *shoes enter his field of vision. They stride over to a mess of debris in the corner of the living room.*

OBJECTIVE SHOT

As GALE *paws through the wreckage to expose the copy of Dr. Spock's* Baby and Child Care. *He grabs the book.*

HI'S POV

The feet walk away and leave his field of vision.

CLOSE ON HI

As we hear the door slam shut with horrible finality.

HI's *mouth stretches wide. He ROARS with grief and frustration.*

WIDE SHOT

Moving down the road toward an oncoming car. As the oncoming car gets closer we can see GALE *and* EVELLE *in its front seat.*

As the car passes we pan with it, to reveal that we have been shooting from the inside of another car, and we hold on the profile of its driver: ED. *She has just watched the other car shoot past.*

ED: . . . Good.

QUICK FADE OUT
INT   DEVASTATED TRAILER

As ED *sits heavily into frame, apparently in shock, her frozen profile to the camera as she stares straight ahead into space.*

Her foreground hand absently holds a length of cord.

Beyond her in the middle background HI *is rummaging in the debris. He stands up, cropped from the chest down and starts loading bullets into the chamber of* ED's *.38 police special.*

HI (*frantically*):   I know you're worried honey but believe me, there ain't a thing to worry about. We're absolutely gonna get him back, there just ain't no question about that . . .

He snaps the chamber shut and leaves frame, still talking.

. . . We'll get him back, that's just all there is to it. And you wanna know another thing?

He is walking back into frame holding another handgun now in addition to the .38, this one an automatic.

. . . I'm gonna be a better person from here on out. And that's final, I mean that's absolutely the way it's gonna be, that's official. You were right and I was wrong . . .

He snaps a clip into the automatic.

HI: . . . A blind man could tell you that. Now they ain't gonna hurt him, they're just in it for the score . . .

HI *is leaving frame again, continuing to talk as we hear him rummaging offscreen.*

. . . But I ain't like that no more, I'm a changed man. You were right and I was wrong. We got a family here and I'm gonna start acting responsibly . . .

HI *enters frame with the two handguns stuck in his belt, holding his pump-action shotgun.*

. . . So let's go honey . . .

He primes the shotgun: WHOOSH-CLACK.

. . . Let's go get Nathan Jr.

TRACKING SHOT

From the front bumper of an automobile. Beautiful desert stretches to the horizon. The road rushes under the camera.

GALE AND EVELLE'S CAR

GALE drives, gazing out at the road. EVELLE holds NATHAN JR., occasionally bouncing him. Contemplatively:

GALE: I luuuuv to drive.

EVELLE: You said somethin' there, pardner.

GALE: . . . Yessir, I figure with the ransom and this bank, you'n I'll be sittin' in the fabled catbird seat.

EVELLE is looking down at the baby, shifting him in his lap.

EVELLE: Uh, Gale . . . Junior had a, uh, accident.

GALE: What's that, pardner?

EVELLE: He had a little accident.

GALE looks over.

GALE: Wuddya mean, he looks okay.

EVELLE: No, ya see . . . Movin' though we are, he just had hisself a rest stop.

GALE: Well it's perfectly natural.

EVELLE (*very excited*):   Hey Gale!

GALE: What now?

EVELLE, beaming, looks up from the baby to GALE.

EVELLE: . . . He smiled at me!

THE SUN

A huge rumbling rippling red ball that fills the frame.

As we hear his footfalls on concrete steps, SMALLS rises into frame, apparently climbing a stoop. The sun behind him throws him into silhouette; the extreme telephoto flattens him against the sun. Heat waves ripple between us and him, making his figure slightly waver.

The rumble builds, louder and louder, until it is snapped off by a—

INT   TRAILER

—CLICK. The front door handle clicks open and SMALLS stands in the doorway. The abandoned trailer is perfectly quiet.

The room is a complete shambles from the fight. Sunlight filters in between the slats of the venetian blinds. Smoke from LENNY SMALLS' cheroot ripples up through the light.

After only a momentary pause at the door to take in the scene, SMALLS goes directly to a specific spot in the debris and nudges some of it aside with his toe, exposing a piece of paper.

He bends down to pick it up but suddenly freezes, with a soft grunt of surprise.

HIS POV

At knee-height on the wall in front of him, "FART" is scrawled in crayon.

BACK TO SMALLS

As he stands up with the piece of paper.

THE PAPER

It is GALE's picture of the Farmers and Mechanics Bank.

INT   CONVENIENCE STORE

Close on a carton of diapers being set down on the check-out counter.

EVELLE (*os*):   Know how you put these thangs on?

WIDER

EVELLE and the CASHIER, a late-middle-aged man (perhaps the proprietor of this small mom-and-pop store) face each other across the check-out counter. EVELLE has various baby purchases—the diapers, baby food, etc.—piled on the counter. The CASHIER is ringing them up.
  Through the open door beyond them we can see a strip of the parking lot.

CASHIER: Welp. Around the butt, then up over the groin area—

EVELLE: I know *where* they go, old timer. I mean do I need pins or fasteners?

We see GALE trotting past through the visible part of the parking lot, cooing "Weeeeee!" as he holds NATHAN JR. up over his head.

CASHIER: Well no, they got those tape-ettes already on there, it's self-contained and fairly explanatory.

EVELLE: Uh-huh . . .

*He takes a plastic-covered squirt gun off a display rack and
drops it on the counter. He is looking around at the other
impulse purchases displayed by the register; he unhooks a bag
of balloons.*

. . . These blow up into funny shapes at all?

GALE is trotting by in the opposite direction: "Weeeeee!"

CASHIER: Well no. Unless round is funny.

EVELLE is pulling a gun out of his belt.

EVELLE: All right, I'll take these too. Now you lie down
back there—

CASHIER: Yessir!

EVELLE: —and don't you move till you've counted up
to eight hundred and twenty-five and then backwards
down to zero. I'll be back to check—see y'ain't cheatin'.

The CASHIER is already down on the floor, out of frame.

CASHIER (os):   You the diaper burglar?

As he heads for the door with the groceries:

EVELLE: Looks like I'm one of 'em.

EXT   STORE

*As EVELLE hurriedly emerges with the two bags. Faintly we
can hear the CASHIER bellowing: "One one thousand, two one
thousand . . ."*

EVELLE: Get the door, will ya?

GALE is slipping the baby back into his car seat, which sits on the roof of the car. He starts doing up the straps.

GALE: He's a real cheerful little critter once he warms up to ya.

Hands free now, GALE reaches for the back door.

EVELLE: Hurry up Gale . . .

GALE has the door open. EVELLE starts throwing in the groceries.

. . . I don't know how high this one can count.

GALE AND EVELLE'S CAR

GALE drives as EVELLE sorts through his purchases.

EVELLE: Got him some baby grub . . . baby wipes . . . diapers, disposable . . . packet of balloons—

GALE: They blow up into funny shapes at all?

EVELLE: No, just—

GALE is looking around, puzzled.

GALE: Say, where's Junior?

EVELLE: Wuddya mean, didn't you put him in?!

GALE: No, I thought—

The two men look at each other.

REVERSE

The two men's heads whip around to look in the back seat.

BACK TO FRONT ANGLE

They look at each other in horror.

GALE: Where'd we leave him?!

The two men's eyes widen as they remember at the same time: both look up at the roof of the car.

CLOSE ON GALE'S FOOT

Coming off the accelerator.

CLOSE ON EVELLE

Screaming as he watches the foot:

EVELLE: NOOOOOO!!

—But too late.

GALE'S FOOT

Already plunging down on the brake. SQUEEEEEEEAL . . .

TWO SHOT

EVELLE *is screaming at the top of his lungs as the car rocks to a stop. He peers through the windshield, still screaming, but nothing has shot off the roof of the car.*

He cranes his neck to look up the slant of the windshield toward the roof. This of course gives him no view; still screaming, he thrusts his body out his open window to look up at the roof. His scream is muted as his head disappears from view, then comes back full force as he ducks back in, frantically shaking his head.

With this GALE's *last hope disappears and he starts bellowing also.*

GALE'S FOOT

Rising from the brake to plunge down on the accelerator.

EXT   THE CAR

As it hangs a squealing U-turn and races off at top speed.

LOW WIDE SHOT

In the foreground NATHAN JR. *sits upright in his car seat, in the middle of the road that fronts the convenience store. He is placidly looking at the scenery.*
   Faintly, we hear the CASHIER *bellowing:*

CASHIER: . . . Seven hunnert ninety-seven one thousand, seven hunnert ninety-six one thousand . . .

GALE AND EVELLE

In their speeding car, both staring out at the road ahead, mouths gaping, emitting ear-splitting screams.

INT   STORE

Shot faces the front of the store with some of the street visible outside. The CASHIER *on the floor is out of frame, but we can hear him loud and clear:*

CASHIER: . . . Seven hunnert ninety-one one thousand, seven hunnert—ah . . . bullshit.

He rises into frame, back to the camera, just as:
   We see GALE *and* EVELLE's *car, through the front window, roaring up the street. Quick as a shot, the* CASHIER *has dropped back out of frame and resumes bellowing:*

. . . Seven hunnert ninety-ought one thousand! Seven hundred eighty—

The car is starting to squeal to a screaming halt.

BACK TO LOW WIDE SHOT

With NATHAN JR. *in the foreground.* GALE *and* EVELLE's *car comes to a rocking halt behind—and inches shy of—the baby.*

EVELLE's *door is already open. He bolts from it and runs over to the baby, blubbering. He picks up the car seat and* NATHAN JR.

GALE *is also getting out of the car.*

EVELLE: Promise we ain't never gonna give him up, Gale! We ain't never gonna let him go!

GALE, *choked up, speaks in a low unsteady voice:*

GALE: We'll never give him up, Evelle. He's our little Gale Jr. now.

HI AND ED'S CAR

HI *driving. Both are staring wordlessly ahead at the road.* HI *looks over at* ED, *glum but trying to be kind.*

HI: . . . Ed, I realize I can't be much of a comfort to you. But lemme just say this . . .

He is nodding to himself.

. . . You'll feel a whole lot better when—

ED: I don't wanna feel better.

HI: Honey—

ED: I don't care about myself anymore. I don't care about us anymore. I just want Nathan Junior back safe.

HI: I know that—

ED: If we don't get him back safe, I don't wanna go on livin'. And even if we do, I don't wanna go on livin' with you.

This shuts HI *up.*
  After a moment:

ED: . . . I guess I still love you Hi; I know I do. I ain't
even blaming you. The whole thing was crazy and the
whole thing was my idea.

  HI *clears his throat.*

HI: Well, factually, I myself bear a very large—

ED: Lemme finish. Since those jailbirds took little
Nathan I been doin' some thinking, and I ain't too proud
of myself. Even if Mrs. Arizona had more'n she could
handle, I was a police officer sworn to uphold the
Constitution of the United States—

HI: Now waitaminute honey, you resigned before
we—

ED: That ain't the point, Hi. We don't deserve Nathan
Jr. Any more'n those jailbirds do. And if I'm as selfish
and irresponsible as you—

HI: Y'ain't *that* bad, honey.

ED: —If I'm as bad as you, what good're we to each
other. You'n me's just a fool's paradise.

FARMERS AND MECHANICS BANK

Baking in the noonday sun.

GALE AND EVELLE

*Sitting in the front seat of their idling car, looking at the
bank.*

EVELLE: There she is.

GALE: Yep. Welp . . .

They look at each other. GALE reaches for his door.

. . . Let's do her.

EVELLE: Waitaminute. What do we do with Gale Jr.?

GALE: Wuddya mean, he waits here.

EVELLE: Are you crazy?! He can't wait here by hisself. Supposin' we get killed in there—it could be hours before he's discovered.

INT FARMERS AND MECHANICS BANK

As GALE and EVELLE bang in through the door. EVELLE holds a shotgun; GALE holds a shotgun in one hand and NATHAN JR. in his car seat in the other.

GALE: All right you hayseeds, it's a stick-up! Everbody freeze! Everbody down on the ground!

Everyone freezes, staring at GALE and EVELLE. An OLD HAYSEED with his hands in the air speaks up:

HAYSEED: Well which is it young fella? You want I should freeze or get down on the ground? Mean to say, iffen I freeze, I can't rightly drop. And iffen I drop, I'm a gonna be in motion. Ya see—

GALE: SHUTUP!

Promptly:

HAYSEED: Yessir.

GALE: Everone down on the ground!

EVELLE: Y'all can just forget that part about freezin'.

GALE: That is until they get down there.

EVELLE: Y'all hear that?

There is a murmur of acknowledgment from all the people on the ground.
    GALE is tossing EVELLE a sack.

GALE: Wanna fill that sack, pardner? We got—shit!

He is looking in shock at the tellers' counter.

. . . Where'd all the tellers go?

There is no one behind the counter.
    A muffled voice from offscreen:

VOICE: We're down here, sir.

EVELLE: They're down on the ground like you commanded, Gale.

GALE: I told you not to use m'damn name! Can't you even try to keep from forgettin' that?!

EVELLE is momentarily abashed, but then brightens:

EVELLE: Not even yer *code* name?

GALE registers understanding.

GALE: Oh yeah . . . m'*code* name.

EVELLE:　　Y'all hear that?

There is a murmur of acknowledgment from all the people on the ground.

GALE:　　All right now everone, we're just about ready to begin the robbery proper . . .

EXT　POLICE CAR

The camera is locked down on the roof of the rocketing squad car, looking past its flashing gumballs.
The car is approaching the townlet, its siren wailing.

BACK TO THE BANK

A teller is finishing stuffing the last of two burlap bags. Close on her hands, we see her putting in a cash packet that is really only a few bills and a sleeve surrounding and hiding a small plastic device.
The teller hits a button on the device and it starts ticking; she shoves it into the sack.

EVELLE:　　All right now everone, you know how this works: Y'all stay flattened for ten full minutes . . .

He is grabbing the two sacks and tosses one to GALE, who also picks up the baby. As the two are backing toward the door:

. . . We might come back in five to check. That's for us to know and y'all to find out.

GALE:　　Anyone found bipedal in five wears his ass for a hat.

They bolt out the door.

EXT　POLICE CAR

Siren jumps in loud at the cut. It is the same locked-down shot over the gumballs.

EXT   GALE AND EVELLE'S CAR

Peeling out from in front of the bank.

INT   GALE AND EVELLE'S CAR

GALE is driving; EVELLE starts pawing through one of the sacks.

GALE: That old timer threw off my concentration. Otherwise it would a gone smoother.

EVELLE: We done okay. Yessir. This ought to split nicely three ways.

A thought registers with GALE and EVELLE at the same moment.
    They look at each other. They both twist frantically to look in the back seat.
    Bellowing:

GALE: Goddamnit! Ya never leave a man behind!

KA-POP! With a loud flat crack something detonates in the front seat and the interior of the car is spattered with bright blue paint.
    GALE and EVELLE, both covered in blue, are screaming in rage, fear and incomprehension. Blue dollar bills snap and flutter around the inside of the car.
    The car is swerving wildly as GALE drives blind, the inside of the windshield covered with blue paint. He reaches forward to wipe clear a patch of windshield.

HIS POV

As the blue paint is smeared away we see HI and ED's car parked broadside in the middle of the road. HI and ED are in front of it, HI aiming his scatter gun, ED her revolver.
    The guns spit orange flame.

HI'S POV

Down the barrel of his shotgun. The car with the blue interior is swerving crazily at us, one front tire blown out.

HI lets go with the other barrel.

The shot chews up the front grill, shatters one headlight and blows out the other front tire. The hood of the car flies open.

The car is squealing to a halt and GALE and EVELLE pile out, still bellowing.

GALE: Goddamnit H.I., ain't we got enough to contend with?

ED is running over to GALE and EVELLE's car, throwing open the back door to look for the baby but coming out only with Dr. Spock's Baby and Child Care.

EVELLE is staggering around in shock, looking in disbelief at his own blue body.

ED: Where's the baby?

EVELLE points this way and that, in a state of confusion.

EVELLE: I think we left him on the roof of the . . . he must be back at the . . .

HI and ED are climbing into their car.

GALE: Let us come with! . . .

HI and ED are already peeling out.

. . . He's our baby too!

CLOSE ON NATHAN JR.

Sitting placidly in his car seat that sits in the middle of the road in front of the bank.

We can hear the wail of the police siren still approaching. As we hold on NATHAN JR. *we hear the distant booming of a shotgun.*

As we boom up to show the empty street beyond the baby, we hear the crack of return fire and furiously squealing brakes. The screech culminates in a loud explosion that snaps off the siren wail. The police car is apparently history.

From beyond the crest of the road ahead a ball of flame has leapt up with the explosion. As the explosion echoes and fades we hear the deep rumble of an approaching engine.

LENNY SMALLS' *motorcycle appears over the rise. Framed against fire and smoke, he is coming directly toward us, and the baby.*

FROM BEHIND HI AND ED

As they top a rise coming from the other direction. We see the baby sitting in the middle of the street, and LENNY *fast approaching from the background.*

LOCKED DOWN TO MOTORCYCLE

The extremely low wide shot, locked down to the speeding bike, shows us rushing toward the rear of NATHAN JR.'s *car seat.*

With a clank of chains LENNY's *hand drops down into frame, palm forward, tensing to scoop up the car seat that we are almost upon.*

A tattoo on LENNY's *wrist reads "No Prisoners."*

REVERSE

Low shot with NATHAN JR. *in the foreground.*

He is scooped up and out of frame as LENNY *roars by.*

ON LENNY

Roaring along. He hooks the car seat over his handlebars.

Randall "Tex" Cobb (Leonard Smalls) on motorcycle

OVER HI AND ED'S SHOULDERS

LENNY is approaching. Under her breath:

ED: What is he?

HI: . . . D'you see him too?

LENNY is sawing a shotgun out of his back holster and leveling it at the oncoming car.
   LENNY is sighting down the gun, swinging it around as he approaches the car.
   HI and ED duck just as:
   The shotgun spits orange flame and the windshield explodes in.
   LENNY roars by.

LENNY'S POV

*The baby on the handlebars in the foreground; the road
rushing by beyond him.*

The bike banks into a hard turn.

FACING HI AND ED

*Shooting through where the windshield used to be, cutting in
at the end of the skid as the car rocks to a halt.*

*HI and ED are raising their heads. Facing forward, they do
not see LENNY approaching again through the rear window.
He is sawing out his second shotgun.*

*HI looks around, reaches and pulls ED down beneath him
just as:*

*Ka-BOOM!—The second shotgun roars and the back
window spits in.*

*As LENNY roars past the back window he casually flips
something in.*

LOOKING DOWN AT HI AND ED

*Folded over in the front seat. Below them something bounces
into and around the leg well—LENNY's grenade.*

EXT CAR

*As the two front doors fly open and HI and ED spill out—HI
from the driver's side, heading for the far side of the road, and
ED from the passenger side.*

ON ED

*As she dives for cover behind a parked car. Beyond her—
KABOOM!—their car explodes and bounces, pouring black
smoke.*

ON HI

*The explosion flings him to the ground in the middle of the
street.*

THROUGH FIRE AND SMOKE

Looking up the street to where LENNY *is wheeling his bike in a U-turn. He is not finished yet.*

HI

Flat on his back, woozily shaking his head.
He weakly raises himself on his elbows to look down the street.

HIS POV

Looking down the length of his own body. His legs stretch away in a V.
Crashing down from a wheelie, LENNY*'s roaring bike is almost upon him—aiming up the middle of the V.*

HI

He rolls. As the bike is roaring by:

HI'S HAND

Reaches and snags a chain on LENNY*'s passing boot.*

HI

Dragged several yards before the boot shakes him off, leaving him on his stomach in the middle of the road.
HI *looks up the road.*

HIS POV

LENNY *is again sluing the bike around.*

REAR WHEEL OF BIKE

Smoking as it skids around in the foreground, completing its turn.
Boom up LENNY*'s back to reveal* ED *stomping straight up the street toward him—unarmed, unafraid.*

ED: I want that baby!

BACK TO HI

He reaches back to pull up his shirt, revealing a gun tucked in his pants in the small of his back. He grabs the gun.

OVER LENNY'S SHOULDER

As ED closes in.

ED: Gimme that baby, you warthog from hell!

LENNY's arms rise into frame. With a roll of his wrists two knives appear in his hands.

BACK TO HI

On his stomach, sighting down the gun toward LENNY.

HIS POV

ED stepping into his line of fire, blocking LENNY.

FROM BEHIND LENNY

Raising an arm to stab.
    ED stoops to scoop the baby from the car seat, revealing: HI, behind her. He fires.

LENNY'S HAND

Drilled by HI's bullet, drops its knife.
    The exit wound spurts, not flesh and blood, but a brief jet of fire.

LENNY

Quick as a flash hurling the other knife at HI.

HI

As the knife stings the gun out of his hand.

KNIFE ON THE GROUND AT LENNY'S FEET

LENNY *bends to scoop up the knife he dropped.*

TRACKING BEHIND ED

As she runs toward the bank, clutching NATHAN JR. *to her chest.*

INT   BANK

As ED *bursts in. The floor is littered with obedient hayseeds.*
  From where he lies prone:

OLD TIMER: Just lie down on the floor, missie.

BANG: The front door bursts open before LENNY's *roaring hog.*
  It sails off a step into the sunken atrium, and lands with a CRASH amidst the hayseeds.

TRACKING BEHIND ED

As she runs for the back door and pushes through it.

TRACKING BEHIND LENNY

As he slaloms through the wildly scattering hayseeds.

EXT   BACK OF BANK

As LENNY *bursts out.*
  With a whipcrack effect he looks left, then right.
  He jerks the bike right, to where an alleyway flanks the side of the bank.

ALLEYWAY

ED *is running up the alley toward the front of the bank as* LENNY *enters. He roars after her.*

LENNY'S POV

Roaring down the alley.

TRACKING IN FRONT OF ED

As the bike approaches behind her.

BACK TO LENNY'S POV

Closing on ED as she reaches the mouth of the alley.
A plank swings into frame, straight at the camera.

REVERSE

Matching action as HI finishes swinging the plank into LENNY's face.
LENNY hits the ground hard as his bike spins out from under him.

THE BIKE

Riderless, twisting crazily into the street where it collapses.

HI AND ED

LENNY is rising to his feet beyond them as HI nods encouragement to ED.

HI: Run along now, honey.

LENNY is reaching back to throw his knife.
HI, unaware, is turning to face him, presenting the plank as—the knife is thrown.
It thunks into the plank, piercing it through.
HI backs up, swinging the knife-studded plank to make LENNY keep his distance.

TRACKING BEHIND LENNY'S SHOULDER

As he reaches up to unhook a chain from a ring on his vest shoulder.

LENNY'S HAND

As the free chain drops down into his palm.

LENNY

Swinging the chain—whoosh whoosh—at the backpedaling HI.

THE PLANK

As the chain snakes around it and rips it out of HI's hands.

LENNY

Grabbing HI by the shirtfront.

LENNY'S OTHER HAND

Swings down and brass knuckles appear on it.

"Tex" Cobb, Nicolas Cage, and Joel Coen

ON HI

As LENNY's *fist swings into frame to club him forehand, then backhand.*

An uppercut from his heels sends HI *sprawling back.*

A PARKED CAR

As HI *lands against it, banging his head. He sinks to the ground.*

LENNY *is casually walking toward him, lighting a cheroot.*

HI *flops over onto his stomach and starts wriggling under the car.*

FROM UNDER THE CAR

HI's *face in the foreground as he desperately seeks escape.*

Behind him we can see LENNY *casually reaching down and grabbing an ankle.*

The shot is framed identically to the shot in the Arizona nursery where HI *pulled a baby from under the crib.*

LENNY *pulls.* HI *is dragged away from the camera and out from under the car.*

HI

Struggling to stand up.

LENNY *wraps his arms around him and applies a tremendous bear hug.*

HI'S ARMS

Crushed against LENNY. *His hands paw futilely at* LENNY's *chest.*

FULL SHOT

LENNY *finally flings* HI *away.*

HI

Landing in the dust, all the fight beaten out of him.

LENNY

Tired of the fight: He saws out both shotguns.

THE HAMMERS

On the guns as LENNY*'s thumbs draw them back. He raises the guns to fire.*

HI

The end of the road.
  He wearily lifts a hand, defensively extending it in front of him—then stops, staring at:

HIS HAND

A hand grenade pin hangs, glinting, from one of his fingers. Pawing at LENNY*'s chest he must have hooked his finger through its ring.*

HI

Reacting.

LENNY

Reacting to HI *reacting. He looks down.*

LENNY'S CHEST

On the bandoliers across his chest, silver pins glint in all the grenades—except one. Its squeeze-lever juts at a right angle from the grenade.

LENNY'S FACE

His jaw drops.

LENNY'S FEET

The lit cheroot hits the ground between his boots.

HI

Scrambling to his feet.

LENNY

Trying to drop the shotguns to free his hands. In his panic his fingers tangle in the trigger guards.

HI

Starting to run.

LENNY

Finally freeing his hands.

HI

Diving behind the parked car.

LENNY'S CHEST

His hands fly in to wrap around the grenade—too late—bright light:

LENNY

Blows sky-high. There is a roar as if the earth were cracking open and flame as if hell were slipping out.
    We pan the fire to the sky.
    Fade out.
    A white aluminum ladder rises up into the blackness, clanking softly. The top of the ladder arcs toward the camera.

JUMP BACK

To the interior of the Arizona second-story nursery as the ladder comes to rest against the window frame.
    It is late at night; the nursery is dark and empty.

THE HEADBOARD

*Of the unpainted crib with the burned-in names: Harry,
Barry, Larry, Garry, and Nathan Jr.*
    As we pull back from the headboard ED's *arms are gently
depositing the sleeping* NATHAN JR. *into the crib.* HI *puts the
singed copy of* Dr. Spock's Baby and Child Care *next to
the baby.*

REVERSE

HI *and* ED *looking sadly down at the baby.*
    *The silence is broken by the bleat of a squeeze-me toy as the
lights are snapped on.* HI *and* ED *turn, startled.*

NURSERY DOORWAY

NATHAN SR. *stands in his jammies, hair disheveled, holding a
gun and squinting against the light.*
    Keeping the gun trained on HI *and* ED, *he slowly raises a
pair of eyeglasses to his nose.*

NATHAN: The *hell* is goin' on?

*He advances cautiously into the nursery, gesturing with his
gun.*

. . . Get away from there.

HI *and* ED *back away from the crib.*
    NATHAN *peers in and studies the baby for a moment.*
    *He lays the gun down, tenderly picks up the baby and
holds him to his chest. A tear forms at the corner of his eye.*
    HI *and* ED *are quietly moving back towards the ladder.*

NATHAN (*sharply*):   Waitaminute . . .

HI *and* ED *stop.*

. . . I ain't through with you. What're you doin' creepin' around here in the dark? You in with Smalls?

HI: . . . Scuse me?

As he bounces the baby, studying HI *and* ED:

NATHAN: Leonard Smalls, big fella rides a Harley, dresses like a rock star?

HI: No sir, that's who we saved him from. It's a long story.

NATHAN: Suppose you tell it.

HI: Well, sir, in a re-ward situation, they usually say no questions asked.

NATHAN: Do they.

HI shrugs.
NATHAN turns to put the baby back in the crib.

. . . All right, boy, I guess you got a re-ward coming. Twenty thousand dollars . . .

He turns around with a thought:

NATHAN: . . . Or, if you need home furnishings, I can give you a line of credit at any of my stores. Fact, that's the way I'd rather handle it, for tax reasons . . .

HI: Well—

NATHAN throws his hands up in the air.

NATHAN: But it's up to you.

HI: Tell you the truth, I think we'd prefer the ca—

ED: We don't want no reward.

HI does a small take, surprised at this much integrity.

. . . We didn't bring him back for money.

NATHAN: Well, we could work it that way too.

ED: Could I just look at him a little bit more?

She stands looking into the crib. HI steps up next to her and puts an arm around her shoulder.

NATHAN: Be my guest, young lady . . . but would you mind tellin' me exactly how you—

ED starts crying softly as she gazes into the crib. HI murmurs something to comfort her.
NATHAN is studying the two of them.

. . . *You* took him, didn't you? Wasn't that biker a'tall.

HI turns to face him. He speaks in a rush.

HI: *I* took him, sir, my wife had nothin' to do with it. I crept in yon window and—

ED (*still crying*): We both did it. We didn't wanna hurt him any; I just wanted to be a mama.

HI: It wasn't for money or nothin'. We just figured you had more'n you could handle, babywise. But I'm the one committed the actual crime sir, if you need to call the authorities—

NATHAN: Shutup boy, no one's callin' the authorities if there's no harm done.

HI: Thank you sir.

ED: Thank you sir.

NATHAN: Aw bullshit. Just tell me—just tell me why you did it.

ED: We can't have our own.

NATHAN looks at her. Finally he nods and sighs.

NATHAN: . . . Well lookit. If you can't have kids you gotta just keep tryin' and hope medical science catches up with you. Like Florence'n me—it caught up with a vengeance. And hell, even if it never does, you still got each other.

HI: Sir, those're kind words. But I think the wife and me are splittin' up . . .

He indicates ED with a nod of the head.

. . . Her point of view is we're both kinda selfish and unrealistic, so we ain't too good for each other.

NATHAN: Well ma'am, I don't know much but I do know human bein's. You brought back my boy so you must have your good points too. I'd sure hate to think of Florence leavin' me—I *do* love her so . . .

He clears his throat and turns to the door. His tone is harder again:

. . . You can go out the way you came in . . .

He snaps off the lights.

. . . And before you go off and do another foolish thing, like busting up, I suggest you sleep on it . . .

He has disappeared into the hall. We hear his voice receding:

. . . at least one night.

HIGH SHOT

Looking straight down at HI, asleep in the trailer bedroom. We start to crane down.

VO: That night I had a dream . . .

EXTREME WIDE SHOT

A beautiful dusk landscape. We are floating in over the field, abutting the prison, that GALE and EVELLE popped out of.
   In the middle background of the extreme long shot two men are walking across the field.

VO: . . . I dreamt I was as light as the ether, a floating spirit visiting things to come . . .

BACK TO HIGH SHOT   BEDROOM

Craning down toward HI.

VO: The shades and shadows of the people in my life wrastled their way into my slumber.

BACK TO FIELD

Still floating forward but now much closer to the two walking men. We see that they are GALE and EVELLE. Both are still dyed blue.
   They are approaching the hole in the ground.

VO: I dreamt that Gale and Evelle had decided to return to prison . . .

EVELLE is starting to climb into the hole.

. . . Probably that's just as well. I don't mean to sound superior, and they're a swell couple guys, but . . .

EVELLE has disappeared and GALE starts climbing in.

. . . maybe they weren't ready yet to come out into the world.

FLOATING UP THE WALK OF THE ARIZONA HOME

The front door has a holly wreath on it.

VO: And then I dreamed on, into the future, to a Christmas morn in the Arizona home . . .

DISSOLVE THROUGH TO:
ARIZONA LIVING ROOM

Five three-year-olds in their pyjamas are opening presents around a tree as NATHAN and FLORENCE look on.

VO: . . . where Nathan Jr. was opening a present from a kindly couple who preferred to remain unknown.

We have been isolating in on one of the children peeling the wrappings off a package marked TO NATHAN JR.
Inside is a shiny red plastic football.

FLOATING IN TOWARD A STATION WAGON

Pulled over on the state highway in the middle of the desert, a police motorcycle parked behind it. GLEN is leaning out the driver's window of the car talking to the state trooper who stands facing him.

VO: I saw Glen, a few years later, still havin' no luck gettin' the cops to listen to his wild tales about me'n Ed . . .

GLEN *is grinning and talking with his hands cupped in front of him, as when he told* HI *about the Pollack who almost stepped in the pile of shit.*
The trooper, in crash helmet and dark sunglasses, is listening tight-lipped and stone-faced as GLEN *finishes his story and slaps his knee.*

. . . Maybe he threw in one Pollack joke too many . . .

The trooper is clicking open his ballpoint pen and reaching his citation book from his breast pocket. The name tag on the pocket says "SGT. KOWALSKI."

. . . I don't know.

FLOATING IN TOWARD A FOOTBALL

It sits on a tee in the middle of a football field.

VO: And still I dreamed on . . .

A cleated foot boots the football out of frame.

. . . further into the future than I'd ever dreamed before.

HIGH SCHOOL FOOTBALL PLAYER

Looking up, arms out at his sides, waiting to receive the kicked ball.

VO: . . . Watching Nathan Jr.'s progress from afar . . .

He catches the ball and starts running.

. . . Taking pride in his accomplishments as if he were our own . . .

He is skillfully eluding and stiff-arming tacklers.

. . . Wondering if he ever thought of us . . .

He reaches the end zone and triumphantly spikes the football. He whips off his helmet and we track in on the face of the rosy-cheeked high-school bruiser.

. . . and hoping that maybe we'd broadened his horizons a little, even if he couldn't remember just how they'd got broadened.

BACK TO BEDROOM

Still craning down, now very close to the sleeping HI.

VO: But still I hadn't dreamt nothin' about me'n Ed. Until the end . . .

DISSOLVE THROUGH TO:
A COUPLE

The man and woman are sitting on a sofa in the foreground with their backs to the camera. They are in the living room of HI *and* ED's *trailer, which is suffused with a warm golden light.*
    As they face the trailer's front door, all we see of the couple is the backs of their heads. They both have white hair, the woman's pulled into a bun. The old man wears a cardigan, the woman a shawl.

VO: . . . And this was cloudier 'cause it was years, years away.

The front door bursts open. Two young couples are entering as their kids—about a dozen of them—stream in around them.

The old couple on the couch raise their arms to embrace their visitors. The children boil onto the couch.

. . . But I saw an old couple bein' visited by their children—and all their grandchildren too. And the old couple wasn't screwed up, and neither were their kids or their grandkids. And I don't know, you tell me. This whole dream, was it wishful thinking? Was I just fleein' reality, like I know I'm liable to do?

FLOATING IN TOWARD A LONG DINING TABLE

In the trailer. The table is all laid out with a Thanksgiving dinner, a huge turkey sitting at the far end.

Cut-out letters at the other end of the room say: WELCOME HOME KIDS!

The grandchildren are running into frame and taking their seats at the table, accompanied by their parents.

VO:　. . . But me'n Ed, we can be good too . . .

The elderly couple enter from either side of the camera and stand in the foreground, backs to us, facing the table.

. . . And it *seemed* real. It *seemed* like us. And it seemed like . . . well . . . our home . . . If not Arizona, then a land, not *too* far away, where all parents are strong and wise and capable, and all children are happy and beloved. . . . I dunno, maybe it was Utah.

The elderly man drapes an arm around his wife's shoulder and draws her close.

She rests her head against his shoulder, and we fade out.